Signs: lettering in the environment

OVERLEAF
RUSSELL COLEMAN, GORDON YOUNG &
WHY NOT ASSOCIATES, *A FLOCK OF WORDS*,
A 300M (328YD) PAVEMENT FROM THE RAILWAY
STATION TO THE SEA, MORECAMBE, LANCASHIRE,
UK 2002

Phil Baines & Catherine Dixon

Signs: lettering in the environment

Laurence King Publishing

Naming places and defining spaces 96

Introduction

Part history, part observation and a large part opinion, this book has been shaped by the other works on this subject that we read as students, by the presentations we have given, the articles we have written and by the discussions we have had with our own students. As a collection of thoughts and images it serves as a record and a celebration of more than ten years of journeys and public lettering discoveries.

Or, put another way, this book is about seeing. It is about seeing the letters which surround us in our public spaces; about seeing that which all too often we don't see: the directional signs for road networks passed by in cars at speed; the inscriptions or names on familiar buildings; even the characters found on the most mundane functional objects of our physical environment such as access grills for public utilities. Such a diversity of material falls outside any one single discipline and includes the work of anonymous letterers, sign-writers, graphic designers, artists, artisans and engineers. What this material has in common, however, is that it all contributes to how our towns, cities and countryside work and, at a more human level, look. While history, architecture and planning all shape the broad picture of our environment, lettering is the most prominent aspect of the detail. And, however much we take this kind of work for granted (and this is no accident), the strategies informing it can be quite complex. So while this book is in part a simple celebration of the fact that such material exists – and a prompt for seeing and noticing more of it as we go about our daily lives – it also provides us with an opportunity for explaining the terms of reference which have focussed our examination of public lettering and which have helped us to understand how and why it works as it does.

Such a study is not without precedent. This book belongs to a tradition of writing about the vernacular within letterforms established during the last century by Nicolete Gray, James Mosley, Alan Bartram and Jock Kinneir. They determined something of the scope of the subject and opened it up to a much wider audience. Certainly, the collection of images and observations gathered here have been shaped by their influence. A few of the places shown will be familiar to any readers who know their books, but these texts are now out of print and a great many of the places/examples recorded have long since disappeared. More recent articles in the design press have continued the tradition of recording examples of letters in the environment, but generally without the kind of critical or contextual discussion we attempt.

This lack of recent discussion has been compounded by shifts in art and design teaching curricula. Ironically, while letters may surround us, nowhere is the subject of environmental lettering taught. Its broad nature means that it is spread too thinly across too many different courses, each with other teaching priorities. In the case of graphic design, a growing emphasis on the typographic has meant that the teaching of the more fluid subject of lettering has all but been abandoned. This, and the ability of contemporary production methods to generate types at any size on virtually any substrate, tends to blind us to the subtle but important differences between lettering and type. Put very simply, type is an industrial product capable of duplication and automation, while lettering is a one-off, created for a specific purpose and capable of responding to the demands of scale, material and surroundings in quite a different way. There are of course exceptions to this definition, but it does provide a broadly useful starting point.

These were then some of the motivations for writing this book. That is not to say however, that this is a 'how to do it' book. Rather in its discussion of practice it aims to provide a broad-ranging and informative resource for practitioners of all kinds, including architects, lettering artists and graphic designers, as well as those who are simply concerned with how and why our environment looks and functions.

37/2

In emphasis this book is intentionally visual. To go back to the underlying idea of seeing, we simply wanted to show as many examples of signs and letters as possible. However, the content is not without narrative or structure. Two primary themes emerge when engaging with this subject, and these form the basis for the major distribution of material across the book.

The first theme is 'signing the way'. It is concerned with those elements from within both our urban and rural landscapes which we would commonly refer to as signs. Here we have documented a range of approaches to basic waymarking and direction-giving for both road-users and pedestrians, as well as sign systems developed for other kinds of travel networks. The second key theme identified is 'naming places and defining spaces'. In this section can be found examples of letters in public spaces which specifically relate to a sense of place and to the role of letters to identify, enliven and record.

123/4

The distinction made between the two primary functions of signing the way and naming places and defining spaces, while helpful, is not absolute. There are areas of some considerable overlap. The signing of stations as part of a travel network identity programme is equally part of an overall strategy for directing travellers and contributes to a sense of place. Street names similarly serve as signs to direct us as well as defining a place.

Each section comprises an introductory essay followed by illustrations arranged thematically and discussed in extended captions. The basis for discussion throughout the book is the function and execution of lettering, and it is these considerations which have informed our selection. As an awareness of context is vital to the ongoing discussions, it is important to note that all the examples shown were photographed *in situ*. Pictures throughout the book are identified by page/picture number. Location captions above the illustrations identify, as accurately as possible, when and where each example was photographed and in some instances (marked †) whether the lettering has since been removed. Contextual dates (in brackets) for construction or execution are included only when felt to be particularly helpful in discussion of the work.

While the book aims to be wide-ranging it cannot, however, hope to be comprehensive; there is just far too much work out there. What is shown directly relates to our own recording methods, determined mainly by where we have been fortunate enough to travel. That said, an awareness of key examples has in some instances directed our paths to designs acknowledged as important. Balanced against many grand examples we have included a body of the far more 'ordinary' kinds as well as many of the most up-to-date examples we could find. History is not forgotten although we make no attempt at a history of the subject. Many historical examples still perform their original purpose admirably and continue to inform the way we interact with our environment, with strange juxtapositions of new and old being an integral part of the contemporary landscape. Pseudo-historical nostalgia, however, is scorned whenever encountered. Our sense of history is rather about identifying a set of practices and traditions which are 'living' and adaptable to the requirements of now, and as such have much to offer the contemporary practitioner and enthusiast alike.

PB & CD

Signs to direct and instruct

Signs should contain only essential information and their significance should be clear at a glance so that the driver's attention is not distracted from the task of driving. ■ Worboys, para.26(c).

40/3

While the term sign can mean a variety of things, many relevant to the broader discussions in this book,* we have used it a little more specifically here to refer to the signs which guide us when going somewhere, whether on foot or bicycle, in a car or using public transport. Such signs have a long history stretching back to Roman times and now form one of the most obvious graphic elements in many towns and cities.

The functions of signs

While we illustrate a wide range of historic examples, our explanation of the various functions of signs focuses upon the kinds of road signs developed after World War II. They are familiar to everyone from a very early age and clearly demonstrate the key design factors to be taken into account.

Signs for roads may be divided into two main groups: 'informatory', that is, direction giving and related information; and 'regulatory', which include all signs giving instructions or warning and prohibiting certain behaviour.

'Informatory' signing

A key role of signs is that of giving directions and related information. Although the exact style of presentation differs from country to country, the principles are generally the same. The information presented by a sign system should be limited to the essentials and should be presented in a consistent manner. It should also be presented at a size suitable for the traffic using that class of road. Unlike the lettering described in the second half of the book, signs do not need to be site-specific, they need to be clearly identified for what they are and stand out from their surroundings. They work by taking into account issues of readability – scale, contrast, letterform – and practicalities such as manufacture and placement.

The scale and ambition of sign systems have a considerable impact on their appearance. While for many people, design is considered a visual activity; – witness the use of the word 'designer' as a prefix to all manner of consumer goods indicating dubious styling of no consequence to the function of the product – design in relation to signing systems is quite different. It is a rational, cerebral activity which involves the analysis and editing of information, the testing of prototypes for legibility under many different conditions, and a knowledge of the manufacturing processes and practices of a considerable number of suppliers.

The editing of information is one of the most crucial tasks in any coherent sign project for it has a bearing not only on its ease of use, but also on the size and therefore cost of the scheme as a whole. Five pieces of information are

* **Sign** *n.* **2 a** a mark, symbol, or device used to represent something or to distinguish the thing on which it is put. **3** a gesture or action used to convey information, an order, request, etc. **4** a publicly displayed board etc. giving information; a signboard or signpost (*Concise Oxford Dictionary*, 1990)

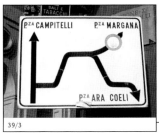

39/3

often thought to be enough to be taken in at any particular moment. On major roads there are clear hierarchies of both signs and the information contained on each. They operate on a drip-feed principle, for example, at the approach to junctions where a sequence of signs spaced half a mile apart give progressively more detailed information before the actual exit.

This approach is common throughout the world, with complicated junctions and roundabouts usually depicted in map form (with the driver at the bottom and 'ahead' at the top) and other kinds of information presented as lists or on arrow-shaped boards.

No less important than the editing of information is the choice of typeface. Having outlined a working distinction between lettering and type in the introduction, it should be clear that the letters used on contemporary signs for transport networks are – despite their scale, material and the way they need to be read – typefaces. In most cases, however, they are specially designed or adapted, and take into account all the variables to be encountered in their application. The variables include the distance from which they need to be read and the movement of the vehicle; the illumination of the sign and the particular manufacturing process used.

Beginning with details first, crucial factors in the design of such faces include the detailing of counters (*ie* the white enclosed spaces within such characters as *b* and *c*); the treatment of ambiguous characters (*eg* capital *I*, lower-case *l* and the figure *1*) and the clarity of numerals.

As with any typeface, the design of the character shapes is only half the job: what helps those shapes to be read easily or not is the space around and between them. Compared to type used in books and general printed graphic design, type on large signs needs more space between characters, words and lines if it is to remain legible from a long distance. In addition to spacing, there is the problem of type printed white out of a dark background, where the white will appear to spread. A common solution here is for there to be two slightly different weights of type, one for 'black-on' and a slightly lighter and fractionally wider-spaced version for 'white-out' use. If signs are to be backlit, yet another variant may be needed.

All this attention to detail will be wasted if the type – when used on signs – is not given sufficient space from the other elements present: the lines indicating roads, pictograms and the border of the sign itself. Examples of both good and bad practice are illustrated.

In the majority of sign systems used for large transport networks since World War II the style of typeface is sans serif. The apparent merits of serifs in knitting words together at sizes used for reading in books do not seem to apply for the sizes used for signs, and the Tyne & Wear Metro* and BAA (see pages 78 & 88–9) are two rare examples of companies which use a seriffed typeface.

The discussion above has assumed signs bearing 'static' information. Today, technology allows for 'active' displays, typically using some form of modular (*eg* dot-matrix) letters whose message is controlled from a central information source. The advantages of this up-to-the-minute information are seen to outweigh the visual shortcomings of the lettering and the amount of

93/3

* The typeface used for this text is Calvert, Margaret Calvert's reworking of her Tyne & Wear typeface. It was released commercially by Monotype in 1985.

13

information which can be given. The quality and reliability of the information is important here, though the initial use in Britain of 'active' displays was as temporary warnings on motorways but a mismatch of information and reality led to them often being ignored. More recent uses have been on public transport networks to indicate the arrival of the next bus (where information is provided from GPS data) or the next train (where the information comes from trackside signals). Apart from the discovery that London Underground minutes are longer than conventional minutes, these provide considerable reassurance to passengers in potentially stressful circumstances.

'Regulatory' signs

56/1

Directional signs for highways are complimented by other signs whose primary concern is with traffic management and road user behaviour rather than destination and geography. There are two main approaches used for this purpose. In the US such signs are predominantly literal but in Europe, symbolic signs have been used since 1931 following the *Geneva convention on the unification of road signals* which was later revised as a protocol in 1949. Signs based on the Geneva Protocol are part iconic, part alphabetic and part symbolic, and its principles are described fully on pages 47–58.

If this standardization across large parts of the world makes it easy for the international traveller to feel at home, its downside is the tendency for everywhere to look the same. Gratifyingly, even within countries which follow the protocol, there is a considerable variation in the drawing and implementation of these signs which allows a little of the characteristics (or aspirations) of individual countries to shine through. In addition, there are several countries which either ignore, or implement only a part of the protocol. Among these are Ireland, Germany and the United States.

Extensive use of symbols, or pictograms, has been argued for many years as it was thought that they could form the basis for an international language which transcended national barriers. More recent research has suggested that pictograms are most effective when they depict the actual thing, but far less so when they represent an idea or concept. This is because ambiguity can creep in when direct visual equivalence is lost. Even basic symbols which we in the West take for granted, for example the pictograms of a man and woman to indicate 'toilets', are understood in other countries simply as 'man and woman'. Because of this, it is now widely accepted that there is no single worldwide symbolic language and so, the use of pictograms must be carefully monitored in situations where the audience is likely to be multicultural.

91/3

Uniformity, diversity and the use of materials

In addition to their functional informational aspect, the provision and design of large scale sign systems can also be a political act. The kind of information that signs carry reflects very much the ideologies of the governments and organizations which erect them as well as the era of their introduction. The signs which greet a traveller at an airport, a ferry terminal or on the roads after a border crossing all have the aim of helping us on our way, but they also become the first words of welcome to that country: 'You can trust me', 'I am modern', or even 'You *will* be robbed'.

20/5

Large signing schemes are introduced ostensibly for the common good, but they often have quite totalitarian overtones. As with corporate identity programmes the implementation of a sign system can be likened to a dog marking its territory. There is a tidy-mindedness which prefers not to tolerate nonconformity. Older signs still exist on minor roads, even in countries such as Britain or France alongside well-planned contemporary systems. They often exhibit a more decorative approach than their replacement models but are usually adequate for the situations in which they are found. Pages 16–21 & 40–3 show some survivors.

One of the recurring themes of this book is that of utility versus personality (or style). This problem is perhaps most present in the issue of signage. While signing systems for roads have an element of neutrality to them, signing on other transport networks has exploited the particularity of letterform or typeface to imbue these functional objects with the role of reinforcing identity.

18/2

While much of the following description of signing presumes the use of typefaces with their implicit consistency of letterform (every 'S' the same, for instance), older forms of transport such as turnpike roads and the early railways had to use lettering, either carved or hand-drawn, if not hand-made. Signs, therefore, relied on the skill of particular makers or workshops, and while they may have had a conformity of spirit they showed a variation in their detailing.

Carving was the earliest durable method of applying lettering and was used on milestones from Roman times onwards. The Industrial Revolution introduced cast iron and an increasing use of patterns and moulds which lent a uniformity to lettering. It is important to remember, though, that casting iron, although an industrial process, was still a small-scale and localized activity. This accounts for the variety of lettering types seen on objects from the eighteenth and nineteenth centuries, and is confirmed by makers' marks which are usually present on even the humblest of items.

20/6

84/6

Other materials exploiting the use of moulds and the principle of modularity were cast terracotta and glazed tile work. Railway companies such as the Underground Electric Railways Company of London* made extensive use of these last two, ensuring that the lettering was an integral part of their stations from 1905 onwards. In 1916, they were the first company to commission what we would now call a 'corporate typeface', Edward Johnston's sans serif, which was manufactured as metal and wood type for use on all notices, names and signing for the company.

* Following amalgamation with the District and Metropolitan railways and various bus operators, this became London Transport in 1933 and is now part of Transport for London.

73/2

Today sign systems are often produced in workshops staffed by workers who understand machines and printing techniques but not letterforms themselves. However, the necessity for well-produced signs has not diminished and designers working in this area of design do seem increasingly aware of both the functional needs of signing as well as the possibilities it can have for reflecting the identity of a particular organization. Rather than using existing typefaces created for print and at far smaller sizes, they commission specially drawn typefaces which take into account both practicalities and social ambitions. New type design formats and software allows this to happen more easily than before, and there is no excuse for badly made signs with illegible type.

Signs to direct and instruct 15

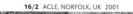

16 Informatory signs: milestones in Britain

The Romans marked distances along their roads with stones called 'milliaries' spaced a thousand paces apart. Examples can still be found even in regions at the very edges of their empire (16/1).

Most surviving milestones or markers in Britain post-date the General Turnpike Act of 1773 which imposed a duty on the various trusts to erect guides at mile intervals in order to charge tolls. In practice, the intervals between these markers often varied as trusts interpreted the distance to their financial advantage, a practice which continued until the mile became a standard measure in 1864.

Shown here are two examples of the more elaborate kind of mile-post. Too grand really for that name, these are important civic features with distance and direction almost an afterthought. The obelisk at Acle (16/2 & 3) was built to commemorate the Silver Jubilee of Queen Victoria and improved in 1980, while the obelisk at St George's Circus (17/1–3) was erected by the Blackfriars Bridge Committee in 1771 as the formal southern termination of a mile-long boulevard leading to their recently completed bridge.

18 Milestones in Britain

A variety of pattern, material and letterform in the treatment of milestones and mileposts is evident on even quite short sections of road. The examples on this page are all from a 20-mile stretch of road and fall into three main categories.

In Cumbria, between Kirkby Lonsdale and Sedbergh (18/1–3), stone is used, painted white with carved and black-painted lettering.

On the long climb from Sedbergh to Kirkby Stephen cast iron is used in and around Cautley, while elsewhere the markers are again made of stone but are of a different style. The road climbs to a height of 336m (1,102ft) and the paint shows the effects of both the exposed setting and weather conditions.

19/4 NEAR ST PAUL MONT PETIT, VENDÉE, FRANCE 2001

19/5 N175 NEAR AVRANCHES, NORMANDY, FRANCE 2001

19/6 KANAGAWA, JAPAN 2002

As with British examples, those in other countries exhibit considerable variety, both in their form and in the kinds of information they convey. Two of the Portuguese examples shown (19/1–2) include full route details, while the third (19/3) does no more than mark progress along the road. In France (19/4) a single figure is used to confirm the road number and the older carved numbers indicating progress are often painted out.

A second example from France (19/5) shows one of the stones erected to celebrate the Allied invasion in June 1944. The Way of Liberty runs from the Normandy Beachhead across Northern France and ends at Bastogne in Belgium.

The final example, from Japan, is clearly contemporary in the materials of its manufacture but follows an age-old strategy in the attachment of a simple panel confirming route and distance to a fixed post.

Kilometre markers: 19
Spain, France and Japan

20 Early British road signs

When the County Councils of England were created in 1889 they assumed responsibility for public highways in their areas but there were no official guidelines about direction signs until the 1920 *Memorandum on road signs and direction posts* which followed the creation of the Ministry of Transport the previous year. This specified details such as the size and colours of posts and lettering but left the exact details open to interpretation by councils and sign manufacturers.

These 'finger posts', as they are generally known, came in a number of materials – cast iron, wood and steel – and in a subtle variety of styles which combine decorative detailing with an overall robustness.

They are comprised of three parts: a pole, the arms and a finial. The poles were seldom plain. Often, wooden examples have carefully chamfered edges and cast-iron poles could be constructed from several sections of different diameters joined by mouldings. The name of the manufacturer was also often included in the casting of the base.

The arms bear the information, which includes the name of the destination(s) in each particular direction and usually the distance.

21/3 LONDON N14, UK 1999

21/4 CAMLET WAY, LONDON EN4, UK 2002

21/5 A151, LINCOLNSHIRE, UK 2002

21/6 B1515, HOLBEACH, LINCOLNSHIRE, UK 2002

Many also carry the A or B road classification numbers first introduced in 1921. The arms were made either from wood with cast letters screwed on to them, or both lettering and arm were cast as a single unit. These arms could simply be bolted to the pole, but many slot over and around it in quite complicated arrangements.

The top of the pole was finished with a finial of some kind. Of these, the most common version is a disc containing the name of the local administrative district. Following the major alterations made to the counties in 1974, these discs often serve as reminders of counties and districts which no longer exist.

Although finger-post signs should all have been replaced following the 1963 Worboys report (see pages 26–31), many local authorities retained them on minor roads where examples can still be found. A Circular from the Department of Transport in 1991 gave them legal recognition once more and encouraged their retention.

Early British road signs 21

22/1 'DIRECTIONAL SIGN' PARK CRESCENT, LONDON W1, UK 1994 †

22/2 'DIRECTIONAL SIGN' CAT HILL, LONDON N14, UK 1999

22/3 'PLACE DIRECTION AT JUNCTION' SUDBURY PARADE/HARROW ROAD, LONDON HA0, UK 1999

22/4 'LANE CONFIRMATION SIGN' WHARFDALE ROAD, LONDON N1, UK 1999 †

22/5 MOTORING ORGANIZATION USE OF STANDARD PATTERN, PRIVATE GARDEN, WELLS-NEXT-THE-SEA, NORFOLK, UK 2001

22/6 'LOCAL DIRECTIONAL SIGN' JUNCTION OF WELL ROAD & B156, HERTFORDSHIRE, UK 2002

22 British 1933/44/57 standard directional signs

In 1933 the Ministry of Transport set up a committee (Maybury) of twenty-six members to examine all aspects of signing. Their proposals established the standard for a national sign system which lasted until 1964. A further committee (Cooke) met in 1944 but only minor amendments were made to the existing scheme.

Directional signs comprised a general background panel upon which was placed smaller information panels and any other graphic elements. The background colour varied according to the class of road: yellow was used for A roads and pale blue for local routes. The information panels, which usually contained the place name used a black all-capitals typeface on a white ground. The A or B Ministry road classifications (introduced in 1921) take precedence over place names. Other signs (22/4) were just black and white, and signs produced by motoring organizations (22/5) followed the standard pattern.

Despite their age, at the time of writing a considerable number can still be seen.

A final revision of the regulations appeared in 1957 and featured an alphabet with improvements by David Kindersley (22/1–4 & 6, 23/2–6).

23/1 RYE, EAST SUSSEX, UK 2000

23/2 HIGH HOLBORN, LONDON WC1, UK 1999 †

23/3 HIGH HOLBORN, LONDON WC1, UK 1999 †

23/4 SOUTHAMPTON ROW, LONDON WC1, UK 1999 †

23/5 THEOBALD'S ROAD/DRAKE STREET, LONDON WC1, UK 1999 †

23/6 PROCTOR STREET/HIGH HOLBORN, LONDON WC1, UK 1999 †

British 1933/44/57 23
standard directional signs

24 British motorway signs: the Anderson committee 1962

In 1957 when the London–Yorkshire motorway (now part of the M1) was under construction, the government set up an advisory committee to look at the problem of signing this new class of road. Chaired by Sir Colin Anderson, reference was made to similar roads in the US and Europe. Practical research was carried out by the Road Research Laboratory in Slough and the Preston bypass (now part of the M6), which opened the following year, was also used to test signs.

The designer, Jock Kinneir, was approached to detail the committee's broad recommendations and was assisted by Margaret Calvert.

The Anderson report recommended a system that was essentially alphabetic, offering directional and distance information designed to be read from 600 feet (183 metres) away. Junctions were to be signed three times with map-type representations, each with differing amounts of information, from the general to the particular. These signs were unusually non-standard in dimension, each being only as large as the information it needed to convey.

Colour was carefully thought out with aesthetic ideals balanced by a consideration of the use of reflective materials and their costs. Black was considered for the background but

it was felt to be too funereal. The blue chosen was the 'American Standard Interstate Blue' which stood out from the countryside and contrasted well with the white type.

Following European and American practice, the committee decided to use upper and lower case type rather than the capital letters used on Britain's roads since 1933. The German DIN lettering was suggested, but was rejected by Kinneir. Wanting a letterform with open counters and clear shapes, he wrote his own specification. Then, finding that the face did not exist, he and Calvert designed one themselves. When revised for the all-purpose roads it became known as Transport. Route numbers were set in the Haas Commercial Grotesque of 1945–6 with amendments made to the figures 4, 6 & 9.

By the time the committee's report was finished in December 1962, eighteen months practical experience had been gained at Preston and twelve months on the M1. That the new signs were deemed a success can be seen by the fact that one year later Parliament had appointed another committee, chaired by Sir Walter Worboys, to recommend signs for all-purpose roads.

**British motorway signs: 25
the Anderson committee
1962**

26 Signs for all-purpose roads in Britain: the Worboys report 1963

The signing for all-purpose roads was a more complex task than the motorways, but many principles established there were able to be extrapolated. The committee which met to discuss this task was chaired by Sir Walter Worboys and Jock Kinneir was again appointed as designer. The signs were of two kinds: regulatory and informatory (principally directional).

While the 1949 *Geneva Protocol* agreed by the United Nations (see pages 47–57)) informed the regulatory signs, it had no comprehensive instructions for directional signs, therefore Kinneir devised a system based on his motorway signs.

Signs used on primary routes have green backgrounds with white type and yellow road numbers. The green was a compromise between the bright green Kinneir proposed and a very dark green suggested by some committee members.

As with the motorways, the idea was to provide information in small amounts and as needed. Junctions were signed either with map-type signs (Kinneir's preferred option) or with stack-type signs. The map-type signs were made more explicit than the motorway versions by the use of lines of differing thickness to denote each road's status. In order to provide information in stages and

to allow the driver time to react, both kinds can be used sequentially at junctions, as shown here.

Colours within the signs were kept to a minimum, white for type and diagram and yellow for road numbers, the relative visual impact of place and route being a reversal of the 1933/44/57 signs.

For the typeface, that used for the motorways was slightly modified and redrawn in two weights: medium (for white and yellow type on dark backgrounds) and heavy (for black type on white). The type was originally produced on tiles rather like the bodies of metal type. These butted up to each other to ensure correct spacing by the many different contractors who were then responsible for the signs' production.

**Signs for all-purpose roads 27
in Britain:
the Worboys report 1963**

28 Signs for all-purpose roads, the Worboys report 1963: directional signs

In addition to the map-type and stack-type signs, simpler signs were used at junctions. Green signs with white type and yellow road numbers were used on primary routes and white signs with black type on non-primary routes.

The message was reinforced here by making the signs themselves arrow shaped and by accentuating that arrow head by placing an arrow within the sign itself. These simple signs, when correctly made and positioned, are very effective.

As before, the map-type signs were laid out as though 'straight ahead' was always at the top, regardless of its true compass orientation.

This sequence of photographs shows how two adjacent urban 'roundabout' junctions are rendered on signs on the various different approach roads.

**Signs for all-purpose roads, 29
the Worboys report 1963:
map-type signs**

30 Signs for all-purpose roads: tinkering with the system

The association of Kinneir and his studio with the Department of Transport lasted no longer than the publication of the report (and even there, the smaller explanatory text plates were not designed by them).

When the *Traffic signs manual* was issued in 1965 several signs had been altered. Among them was the way road numbers were shown on non-primary route signs.

In Kinneir's original proposals place names and road names were simply set in black and allowed to speak for themselves. From the first applications of the signs, however, an attempt was made to reinforce the numbers by the addition of a coloured panel to denote when a route was 'primary' (an A road is not necessarily primary).

30/1 shows a particularly ugly example of this idea in practice (as well as it being an example of two transport organizations not talking to each other about siting their respective signs).

Following experiments in the Guildford area in 1989, the 1994 regulations introduced a more dramatic way of indicating the class of road that a particular destination was reached by. On the opposite page is the same sign as 30/1, now showing local destinations and with the large coloured panels of the

1994 regulations. The most legible element of the sign is no longer the diagram closely followed by the type, but the series of coloured boxes. They upset the visual balance of the sign, confuse the eye and destroy the sense of the junction which the diagram was intended to convey.

The other pictures here show more examples of the 1994 regulations in use. Note how, on the green primary route signs, destinations reached along minor roads are the most dominant visual aspect of the sign.

Since 1994 there has also been an increasing tendency to use coloured backgrounds (31/2 & 3) to surround signs, presumably to increase their target value. In few cases do these ever seem to be necessary, although grey is definitely the lesser of two evils. Yellow can only be described as an aesthetic and environmental disaster.

Signs for all-purpose roads: 31
tinkering with the system

32/3 MONTSERRAT AERI, SPAIN 2002

32 International use of the Transport alphabet

The British Department of Transport's manual, which contained the guidelines for the Kinneir Calvert signing system, was bought by many other countries and aspects of it can now be seen across the globe. In some countries the basic design for directional signs was adopted (opposite/3 and following pages) with allowance for an additional language.

In others, the typeface alone was used on signs of their own design. Kinneir and Calvert's typeface, known as Transport, has never been commercially available (apart from appearing on Letraset sheets in the 1960s and 1970s). The various other versions of it, and the derivative italic (see next page) and Greek display varying degrees of fidelity to their original design.

↑ 41 Seltjarnarnes 3
P Rvk-Gamla höfn

← P Rvk-Tjörn

↰ P Kolaport

↑ P City Nord-Øst
347 Frie pladser

→ P City Vest
406 Frie pladser

Οσιος Δαβίδ
Μονή Λατόμου
Osios David
Monastery of
Latomou

International use of 33
the Transport alphabet

34 International use of the Transport alphabet: bilingual road signs

Following on from the previous spread, here are further examples of international signs which make use of the Transport alphabet. These examples also feature a range of strategies employed to clearly manage bilingual information and the maintain a visual equality between two languages.

In Saudi Arabia the sheer visual difference of the scripts used provides a clear distinction between the English and Arabic which is further reflected in the left and right alignment of each.

In Greece there is visually far less difference between the two scripts and so colour is used as the main mechanism of differentiation. The examples shown also highlight the importance of spacing – the legibility of (34/4) being compromised by having far too little.

In Ireland the management of the English and Irish texts is severely compromised by neither one making the best use of the Transport alphabet. Instead of using the strongest upper and lower case setting, English is set in all capitals and the Irish in an italic variation.

International use of 35
the Transport alphabet:
bilingual road signs

36 **The US 'Interstate' type**

The system of signs used on American roads was one of several looked at by British engineers and Jock Kinneir in the late 1950s.

As already mentioned, the decision to use upper and lower-case setting of words was based on the belief that it creates more distinctive word shapes. Tests in California in 1950 and Germany in 1957 had suggested as much.

American directional signs feature a distinctive typeface with generous inter-character spacing. There are several characters with easily recognized features. The tail on *g*, the diagonal termination to the uprights of *d*, *h*, *l*, etc. In older versions, the letters are infilled with reflective studs (36/1).

Like the British Transport alphabet, this typeface has travelled (37/3–5) and undergone modifications along the way. In 1993–4 it was digitized by Tobias Frere-Jones and made commercially available by the Font Bureau. It is now widely used by graphic designers world-wide for purposes far removed from its origins. Although the American type was used for many years in the Netherlands (37/5) it has recently been replaced by type designed by Gerard Unger.

Not all countries subscribe to the idea of superior upper and

37/1 BOSTON, MASSACHUSETTS, USA 1999

37/2 LORETTO, MINNESOTA, USA 2002

37/3 CAMPS BAY, CAPE TOWN, SOUTH AFRICA 2002

37/4 KUALA LUMPUR, MALAYSIA 2000

37/5 & 6 THE HAGUE, THE NETHERLANDS 1996

lower-case legibility, however.
France is one such place and some
recent signs are shown on pages
44–5. Another use of all-capitals
is this older Dutch sign (37/6)
which uses a generic industrial
sans serif letterform.

Pg. Sant Joan

Pl. Joanic

Pl. Joan Carles I

C. Mallorca

Diversion For Vehicles
Below 5.5 Tonnes
五公頓半以下車輛改道

High Street
高街

First Street
第一街

Queen's Road West
皇后大道西

P.ZA MARGANA

VIA DELLE
BOTTEGHE-OSCURE

V. DEI POLACCHI

3429

357G

38 **Map-type direction signs: Spain, France and Italy**

The use of map-type directional signs in Britain has already been described on pages 26–7 & 29. Their use is widespread but unlike the Geneva Protocol signs (see pages 47–59) there is no uniformity across countries. Those shown here are from different countries and cover a span of about forty years.

The success of these signs depends firstly on the relationship between the drawing and the road being believable and secondly on the information being presented in a comprehensible quantity. Apart perhaps from (38/3), all the signs shown on this spread fail one or other of these requirements.

VENDÉE

CHALLANS 17 →
Gc 21
· Gc 107 · St MAIXENT

VENDÉE

St MATHURIN 5 →
Les SABLES D'O 8 →
St MARTIN DE B
← 7

VENDÉE

Vo
AIZENAY
← 11

VENDÉE

Gc 87
La FORÊT D'OLONNE
← 4

VENDÉE

Gc 107
APREMONT
← 7

40 Michelin signs in France

The need for comprehensive signing for roads was recognized in France as early as 1912 by groups such as the National Office for Tourism, the Touring-Club de France and the Department for Bridges & Roads. In 1920 a circular identified that such signs had to give directional and distance information; be legible at a great distance both at night and during the day; and be durable.

Edouard and André Michelin, founders of the French tyre company, experimented with designs based on surviving Roman milestones and eighteenth-century 'borne' from the Route Royale. 'Borne Michelin' (kilometre markers or indicators) were the resulting bollard forms (41/1–5) which were made of concrete and first appeared around 1931. Other designs were named 'Plaque Michelin' (40/1–6) and 'Poteau Michelin' (posts; 41/6).

Around 70,000 of the different kinds of markers were produced by the company until 1970. Usefully, their glazed ceramic information panel carries a date and reference number in the same way that the reverse of many modern signs have some form of identifying label to indicate date and manufacturer.

In arrangement, the clear conveyance of information on all these

signs is compromised by the need to fit it within a determined area. In spite of this, however, there is a recognizable hierarchy: the road numbers, where applicable, are given priority; and the department name – Vendée – is accentuated by the reversed-out panel when on a classified road. (The roads classified GC on all these examples are marked D on modern maps, VO is an unclassified road.)

Some may consider them to be too 'decorative' today, but with their distinctive appearance (especially when well maintained and painted white) and predictable siting, they still function efficiently, especially on roads where speed is not the primary consideration.

Michelin signs in France 41

42/5 & 6 ST JEAN DE MONTS, VENDÉE, FRANCE 2001

42 Michelin signs in France

The Michelin signs used from the 1950s onwards follow a basic design which can be seen as an enlarged variation of the 'poteau' of the previous page. Here, though, the form of the sign assumes a much greater importance. The sign itself is an arrow reinforcing the graphic element of the tapered blue arrowhead. As before, the information takes the form of glazed ceramic panels, dated on their bottom right-hand corner, which were mounted onto pre-cast concrete stands of a standard pattern. On the reverse, Bibendum (42/6) is cast into the concrete together with the date of manufacture.

These later signs exhibit a far more rational approach to the management of information, with differing sizes and weights of lettering used to denote the relative importance of destinations. The signs also vary in size according to the relative quantities of information they need to convey.

In addition to general directional road signs, versions also exist for the needs of tourists and these use an italic seriffed letterform (43/3, 5 & 6). Geneva Protocol signs were also made in 'poteau' versions and one can be seen on page 53 (53/3).

QUIBERON
PORT-LOUIS
LORIENT

D 119

PLŒMEL 8
AURAY 12

43/3 & 4 AURAY, BRITTANY, FRANCE 2002

QUIBERON
CARNAC
PORT-LOUIS

CRACH
LOCMARIAQUER
Sᵗ PHILIBERT
LA TRINITÉ

*Route
Touristique*

HENNEBONT
LORIENT
PONTIVY

*Rampes du Loch
Vue sur le Port
Piétons - Seulement*

Site de Sᵀ GOUST

*Chapelle
N.D. des Fleurs*

44 France after Michelin

The basic form of the later Michelin signs continued to be used in France until only recently.

The distinctive tapered arrowhead was retained, as was the practice of using several signs rather than the more elegant but less flexible practice of combining information on a single larger sign.

The earliest examples here (44/5 & 6) are primarily aimed at tourists and use the same serif typeface which features on the equivalent Michelin signs. The others are far more uniform, using sans serif with tourist information in italics.

In contrast to many other countries, and certainly to accepted British theory, these latest French signs (45/1–3) are set in all capitals. The only time such signs become difficult to decipher, however, is when the letterspacing varies from one line to the next as happens in the sign in Auray (45/1).

It is also worth noting that these signs use only a limited number of standard sizes rather than allowing the overall size to be dictated by the quantity of information.

Whatever they lack in design subtlety, it is probable that in this latest incarnation – of fixed sizes and in articulated panels – errors will not be nearly as apparent as with other systems.

45/1 AURAY, BRITTANY, FRANCE 2002

45/2 'ADVANCE WARNING OF JUNCTION' A16, ARTOIS, FRANCE 1998

45/3 JUNCTION OF D32 & D54, VAIRÉ, VENDÉE, FRANCE 2000

46 Highlighting road numbers

One way of limiting the information on a sign is to use route numbers rather than destinations. This is often combined with a colour-coding of the various road classifications. Some examples have been discussed on previous pages.

Those shown here represent two further approaches. Those from the US (46/3) merely confirm to the traveller the route number and serve primarily to reassure.

The examples from Sweden and Poland (46/2 & 4) show signs which contain coloured patches within a larger sign. Apart from 'Centrum', the sign from Sweden dispenses with destinations altogether, but the fussy detailing of the box borders does little for legibility at a distance. In the Polish example the destination is given priority while the inset panels are helped by being more distinctively coloured than those from other countries.

The directional signs shown on the preceding pages show considerable national differences. There is, however, much more agreement about the smaller and more common warning and instructional signs used on road networks. Certainly, most European countries have signs which adhere to – or

share a close relationship with – the 1949 Protocol resulting from the UN world conference on road and motor transport held in Geneva.

In the protocol there are three basic kinds of traffic signs; signs to warn, signs to prohibit and signs to instruct. The treatment of shape

and colour of each plays an important role in differentiating between them and conveying their message.

While this protocol described signs in terms of their form, content and colour, it did not address more specific details of their appearance. So, in addition to the different styles of drawing to be

found on these signs, there exists considerable variation in the treatment of border widths and the inventiveness of methods used to mount a sign onto a pole.

Regulatory signs: 47
the Geneva Protocol 1949

48/1 'CROSSROADS' NEAR NOTRE DAME DE RIEZ, VENDÉE, FRANCE 2001

48/2 'TWO-WAY TRAFFIC' ST HILAIRE-DE-RIEZ, VENDÉE, FRANCE 2001

48/3 'ROAD NARROWS ON LEFT' NEAR SEDGWICK, CUMBRIA, UK 2000

48/4 'ROAD HUMPS' CAPE TOWN, SOUTH AFRICA 2002

48/5 'UNEVEN ROAD' NYÄNGSVÄGEN, STOCKHOLM, SWEDEN 2002

48/6 'CAMELS' NAD AL SHEBA, DUBAI, UNITED ARAB EMIRATES 2002

48 Geneva Protocol: signs which warn

Shown on this spread are some of the triangular signs which are used to warn. These have a black pictogram on a white ground framed by a red border – red is the widely accepted colour for both warning and emergency.

In some countries the background is yellow rather than white in an effort to make them still more noticeable. Even blue has been used, see the older example of a warning sign from South Africa (48/4).

This same example also illustrates the way that a sign system will evolve over time. As driving practices change so new pictograms are arguably needed – in this instance the uneven road sign (48/5) has been adapted to indicate the presence of speed bumps.

Simply through use, refinements are made. The exclamation mark as a general indicator of hazards, for example, is now widely favoured over the original sign showing a vertical bar (49/3 & 6).

Yet, there is still much to be said for the simplicity of early protocol. Animal hazards were originally to be indicated by the use of a generic sign but are now represented by a large number of pictograms differentiating individual species. While reference to specific animal hazards can add a very distinct

49/1 'PEDESTRIAN CROSSING' AL SAFA, DUBAI, UNITED ARAB EMIRATES 2002

49/2 'LEVEL CROSSING WITH BARRIER' ST HILAIRE-DE-RIEZ, VENDÉE, FRANCE 2001

49/3 'OTHER HAZARD: WHITE LINE PAINTING' ITALY 2002

49/4 SEOUL, KOREA 2002

49/5 'SLIPPERY ROAD: ICE' VASTO, ITALY 2002

49/6 'CAUTION: BLIND HILL' GRINDAVÍK, ICELAND 2001

flavour to one's travelling experience of a country, the overall effect of too many signs in any one country confuses rather than clarifies.

Rectangular information plates can be used in situations where further clarification is needed.

50 Geneva Protocol: signs which warn

The protocol did not describe signs in terms of the details of their drawing, thus they show considerable national differences in terms of sensitivity of line and technical ability.

The style of the first example (50/1) is similar to the 1933 & 1944 British model in the use of a warning triangle accompanied by a separate information panel below to denote a specific danger or hazard. However, the drawing itself is closer in spirit to the early protocol, with the depiction of a single child rather than two.

Though adhering more closely to protocol, the other examples on this page show how treatment of the same basic sign can differ in practice. Drawing style and attention to detail is hugely inconsistent, both between examples and even within individual signs. In one of the two signs from Barcelona children are shown to carry bags but have no feet (50/2).

Note how the general protocol for the likely presence of children in the road is qualified with a rectangular warning plate.

Even in those pictograms less directly pictorial in representation it is still possible to find huge variation in the treatment of line alone. (51/1 & 4).

Some of the national differences in the interpretation of different

signs are not as arbitrary as they might at first seem. The placement of a pictogram within a space can carry with it a directional implication. The examples of the warning signs for children and the above example of the sign for roadworks ahead (51/2) all suggest that the particular hazards in question might threaten from the right to left. This is in accordance with the Continental practice of driving on the right side of the road. In countries where this practice is reversed, such as Britain, the images on the signs are also reversed (51/5).

Sometimes local interpretations of warning signs represent a rare step beyond protocol altogether and, as the example shows, can be charming and no less effective (51/3 & 6).

Geneva Protocol: 51
signs which warn

52/4 'NO BIKES' & 'NO SKATEBOARDS' CAPE TOWN, SOUTH AFRICA 2002

52/5 'NO GOODS VEHICLES' & 'NO BUSES' VASTO, ITALY 2002

52/6 'NO MOTOR VEHICLES' HONG KONG, CHINA 2002

Appelviksvägen 40-2

escluso carico e scarico

Except with permit
有許可証者
不在此限

52 Geneva Protocol: signs which prohibit

In the protocol, circular signs which are predominately red or which have red borders give negative (prohibitory) orders and, as with the warning signs, there are considerable variations of drawing style, border width and method of fixing.

The use of the diagonal bar to cross out the pictogram (implying the prohibition more strongly) has varied over the years. The sign from Hong Kong (52/6), for instance, shows the 1964 GB version of the protocol, in current British regulations the diagonal has been abandoned for all except the 'No left turn', 'No right turn' and 'No U-turn' signs.

Another aspect of the prohibitory signs to have noticeably changed with the times has been the representation of vehicles. A contemporary idea of generic vehicles is maintained on the signs although again, visual representation will differ between countries. Italy, for example, favours a stencilled approach to the depiction of their vehicles and especially the buses and lorries (52/5), while in Greece the images presented are altogether more robust and solid in appearance (53/4).

53/4 THESSALONIKI, GREECE 2002

53/5 'NO LEFT TURN' HONG KONG, CHINA 2002

53/6 'NO ENTRY' THORNILDSPLAN, STOCKHOLM, SWEDEN 2002

Geneva Protocol: 53
signs which prohibit

**54 Geneva Protocol:
signs which instruct**

The Geneva Protocol circular signs with white diagrams on a blue background are mandatory, they give positive instructions.

Blue is also the background colour for white arrows in many countries (see pages 60–1) as well as a general colour for the rectangular warning plates used with the

diagrammatic signs to amplify their meaning.

55/1 'STRAIGHT AHEAD OR RIGHT ONLY' THESSALONIKI, GREECE 2002

55/2 'TURN LEFT OR RIGHT' CROIX-DE-VILLE, FRANCE 2001

55/3 'PASS EITHER SIDE' PIAZZA GANDHI, EUR, ROME, ITALY 2002

55/4 'DESIGNATED PEDESTRIAN ROUTE' STOCKHOLM, SWEDEN 2002

55/5 'MINI-ROUNDABOUT' THESSALONIKI, GREECE 2002

55/6 'SEPARATED CYCLE & PEDESTRIAN PATHS' COPENHAGEN, DENMARK 1998

CÉDEZ LE PASSAGE

YIELD

止まれ

STOP

N 9th Av

N Washington Av

STOP

STOP

56 Geneva Protocol: signs with non-standard shapes

Certain signs are of non-standard shapes to give them greater prominence, for example, the 'give way' or 'stop' signs.

The unique inverted triangular shape of the original protocol for the 'slow major road ahead'/'give way' sign was believed to make enough of a visual statement to distinguish such an important sign from all the others. However, subsequent interpretation has also seen qualification of the individual shape through the addition of words.

The example shown from Ireland (56/2) reflects the Anglo-American influences prevalent in the signage of that country in its combination of US English text within a protocol format (see also page 34).

The 'stop' sign from Spain (56/4) is the 1949 protocol version which became part of the British 1964 regulations. It has since been replaced by the octagonal pattern which originated in the United States and has the virtue of being less ambiguous and having a more distinctive shape. It was introduced into the British regulations in 1975.

57/1 SEOUL, KOREA 2002

57/2 PRAGUE, CZECH REPUBLIC 1994

57/3 REYKJAVIK, ICELAND 2001

57/4 KANAGAWA, JAPAN 2002

57/5 CAPE TOWN, SOUTH AFRICA 2002

57/6 OPORTO, PORTUGAL 2001

No specification for notification of a pedestrian crossing is provided in the Geneva protocol. As the need for such a sign has grown, so various adaptations on the basic idea for signs which warn (see pages 48–51) have emerged. In some instances the basic triangular shape of the warning signs has been distorted in the creation of a rather odd polygonal shape (57/1 & 4). Elsewhere, though, a certain kind of homogeneity has been achieved by reversing out the triangular shape from a blue rectangular background. The colour of the triangle – yellow or white – seems to correspond to the background treatment of the other signs in a given country's system.

As for the representation of the pedestrian himself – and for the most part it surely is a him – there seems to be little rational explanation for why the wearing of a hat should feature in the depiction of the crossing of a road.

Geneva Protocol: 57
adaptations & expansion

58 Other standards: the US diamond pattern

In the US there seems to be a certain distrust of the European symbolic approach to signs and a much greater reliance on words to either convey the message or to repeat it.

Although a few US signs – such as the 'No entry/Do not enter' sign (58/1) – are the same as that of the Geneva Protocol, the warning signs are of a quite different pattern. These yellow diamonds are distinctive mainly by virtue of their colour and shape rather than the quality and clarity of the typography or illustrations they carry.

Their use is not confined to the US, and shown here are examples from the Far East and Ireland.

Ireland's road signage is a curious mixture with directional signs based on the British Worboys model (see pages 26–9); signs based on the Geneva Protocol; signs based on the US diamond pattern and an idiosyncratic 'No entry' sign. When used for roadworks the diamond is coloured orange rather than yellow. 59/6 shows a perverse approach to the problem of making the diamond into a rectangular temporary self-supporting sign.

59/4 WASHINGTON AVENUE NORTH, MINNEAPOLIS, MINNESOTA, USA 2002

59/5 DUBLIN D7, IRELAND 2002

59/6 SIR JOHN ROGERSON'S QUAY, DUBLIN D2, IRELAND 2002

60 Variations on a theme: arrows

The treatment of even simple motifs such as arrows differs widely. The Geneva Protocol of 1931 shows triangular serifs with tapering shafts, examples of which can still be found in older signs such as the example shown from Greece (60/3).

The 1949 protocol for mandatory instructional signs favoured arrow-heads more barbed in appearance, although still with a tapered shaft. Now, most arrows reflect a varied approach to the arrowhead itself but generally have a shaft with parallel sides. As can be seen from the range of examples shown here, careful consideration needs to be given to the relationship between line width, length and the size of arrowhead as these factors affect clarity and overall impact.

In his consideration of the signs for the all-purpose roads in Britain (see pages 26–31), Jock Kinneir contributed much to the rationalization of the visual treatment of the arrowhead across a given system. He rejected the use of the arrowhead within his directional signs on the grounds that they were too heavy and contributed to a certain visual untidiness. Instead, Kinneir realized that with a line of sufficient strength a chamfered end would be clear. This idea was then followed through in the treatment

ΔΕΥΤΕΡΑ - ΠΑΡΑΣΚΕΥΗ
MONDAY - FRIDAY
06³⁰ - 20³⁰

ZONA
TRAFFICO
LIMITATO

Ensrettet

Gælder ikke

ZETAZEROALFA

of arrows in both the warning and prohibitory sign categories, in effect tidying up inconsistencies present in the 1949 protocol (see pages 47–57). Kinneir recognized, however, that arrowheads were an unavoidable aspect of the mandatory signs where direction often needs to be emphasized. Here,

the potential for blockiness in the treatment of the arrowheads was overcome simply by increasing the degree of barb which lightened the overall visual effect (60/2).

Other examples show how a tendency toward over-emphasis in our signing – either through the repetition of message in both

symbol and text or through over-signing – can add to the visual noise which surrounds us and not to any sense of clarity.

**Variations on a theme: 61
arrows**

62 **Using the road**

Because town and city streets are frequently crowded with an array of signs, fascias and advertisements all vying for attention, highway authorities often make use of the road itself to direct and otherwise give messages.

The most typical method is by painting or, less commonly, by stencilling with a durable and often reflective paint. In order to make such messages legible from the driver's perspective, such signs appear elongated when viewed from above.

64 Using the road

There is an even greater variety of drawing and painting skills evident in the way symbols are painted onto roads than in any other aspect of signing.

While some of the examples here would doubtless concern the highways engineer, they are all understandable as symbols and their inadequacies are more likely to put a smile on the face of passers-by.

Where the paved surface is not tarmac but cobbles or some other modular units, the possibilities of using contrasting materials as part of the pavement itself becomes a possibility. There is no loss of clarity in this method (65/1 & 2) and it is always visually superior to covering over such a surface with paint (see also pages 138–9). Imagine how good 'yield' on the previous page (63/5) would have looked if made out of contrasting paving blocks.

65/3 & 4 show a more formal use of the ground as part of a much larger signing project in the recent regeneration scheme for London's Bankside area. Clever use is made of the pavement to direct people towards key local sites. These directional signs are made from inlaid terrazzo blocks and were designed by Richard Hollis for the design group Muf.

KEEP CLEAR

SOUTHWARK CATHEDRAL

BOROUGH MARKET

TATE

GALLERY OF MODERN ART

66/1 LOUTH, LINCOLNSHIRE, UK 1992

66/2 ST MARTIN'S PLACE, LONDON WC2, UK 1999

66/3 UPPER GROUND, LONDON SE1, UK 1993

66/4 QUEEN VICTORIA STREET, LONDON EC4, UK 1993

66/5 ABOVE RIVERSIDE WALK, LONDON SE1, UK 1993

66/6 RIVERSIDE WALK, LONDON SE1, UK 1999

66 Signs for pedestrians: heritage & modernity

Increasingly, there is a perceived need for comprehensive signing within urban areas, and this is often connected with the tourist industry.

The British road sign system is little used in a pedestrian context despite allowance in the regulations for signs of a reduced size for this purpose, an example of which can be seen in 66/1. The solution favoured by many local authorities are these retro finger posts (66/1–3) whose fussy detailing shows a lack of real appreciation for the robust straightforwardness of so much of Georgian and Victorian design. Sadly, they also fail at a practical level: the type is too small and tightly 'set' for reading across a wide road.

Not all contemporary approaches are successful though. The City of London's signs (66/4) exhibit an admirable lack of retro-heritage styling and would be models of clarity if they could only lose a few symbols. Examples from London's South Bank (66/5) erected in the 1970s and modelled on French road signs of the period are uncompromisingly of their time but are simply too large in scale and visually overbearing. They also follow an unfathomable colour code.

A fresher approach can be seen in the sign system for the South Bank

Centre (66/6) by CDT Design Ltd. The signs themselves are positive and appear contemporary, though clear message-giving is enlivened by a subtle evocation of the past courtesy of the Skylon-inspired stainless steel mast shape. Our only criticism would be the unadventurous choice of (Swiss) typeface.

What is clear from many of these pedestrian signs is that they are produced by people who don't seem to know or care about how to manage words and their meaning. 67/1 shows words assembled without any appreciation of the necessary relationship of space between words or lines: the sign can be too easily misread as directions to 'Post St Library' or 'Albert Coach Old'.

67/2 has tackled the problem by making the lettering the dominant visual element by use of colour and size. And while appearing traditional, the detailing of the post and arms is also considerably better handled than 66/2 & 3 and 67/1.

The final example is again a more contemporary design and shows the benefit of a careful consideration of layout. The definite space for pictograms and arrows prevents either from affecting the primacy of the words.

Signs for pedestrians: 67
heritage & modernity

68 **Signs for pedestrians: rural simplicity**

Signs on footpaths, in rural areas or in parks often exhibit a clarity and simplicity missing in many of their urban counterparts.

69/1 LAMBRIGG FELL, CUMBRIA, UK 2001

69/2 TABLE MOUNTAIN, CAPE TOWN, SOUTH AFRICA 2002

69/3 RIDGE, HERTFORDSHIRE, UK 2002

69/4 ALIGNMENTS DU PETIT-MENEC, BRITTANY, FRANCE 2002

69/5 NEAR PREBENDS BRIDGE, DURHAM, UK 2000

69/6 COPENHAGEN, DENMARK 1998

Signs for pedestrians: 69
rural simplicity

70/3 PIAZZA DI PIETRA, ROME, ITALY 2002

70 **Signs for pedestrians: over-design**

In addition to basic navigational signing, there is also a need for other, more explanatory, signs to inform about specific places.

The three examples on this spread show designs whose effectiveness is compromised for different reasons. 70/1 is simply too self-conscious, a designer's misguided conceit. 70/2 has far too much information set in type far too tightly set (long lines with too little space between them) for reading while standing in a public place. The inclusion of two languages is laudable, but only a severe editing of both text and images could allow scope for a successful redesign.

70/3 & 71/1 show one of a number of bronze stele from Rome. Their form is distinctive and their bilingual approach and consideration of the visually impaired is again to be praised. They also feature a typeface, Scipio by Giovanni Lussu, which is an interpretation of second-century engraved letterforms from Rome. They are, however, incredibly difficult to read because the interlinear space (leading) is considerably less than their word space making it hard to follow the lines of text. This fundamental error hinders the effectiveness of an otherwise well-considered piece of street furniture.

PAPA INNOCENZO XII L'EDIFICIO PER LA DOGANA DI TERRA,
CON L'INGRESSO IN ASSE AI RESTI DELLE COLONNE.
NEL 1870 L'EDIFICO VIENE RINNOVATO E DESTINATO ALLA
BORSA VALORI E CAMERA DI COMMERCIO.
NEL 1925 IL BASAMENTO E LE COLONNE VENGONO ISOLATI
CON VNO SCAVO CHE ESALTA LA PRESENZA DEL TEMPIO.

THE TREVI-PANTHEON ROVTE PASSES THROVGH PIAZZA DI
PIETRA, THE PROPORTIONS OF WHICH DERIVE FROM THE SPACE
WHICH ONCE SEPARATED A TEMPLE DEDICATED TO HADRIAN,
CONSTRVCTED IN THE II CENTVRY A.D., FROM THE PORTICO
WHICH SVRROVNDED IT. THE TWO LONGITVDINAL WALLS
COINCIDE WITH THE REMAINS OF THE TEMPLE'S ELEVEN
COLVMNS AND WITH A ROW OF BVILDINGS BVILT ON THE
REMAINS OF THE PORTICO. THE ROVTE ARRIVES AT PIAZZA DI
PIETRA VIA LATERAL PATHS WITH RESPECT TO THE TEMPLE
AND THE VNEXPECTED PRESENCE OF THE MONVMENTAL
REMAINS FORCES THE VISITOR TO DEVIATE FROM HIS PATH IN
ORDER TO APPRECIATE THE GIGANTIC ORDER OF THE COLVMNS.
THE VSES TO WHICH THE REMAINS OF THE TEMPLE HAVE BEEN
PVT IN MODERN TIMES CAN BE ORDERED INTO THREE PRINCIPAL
PHASES. AT THE END OF THE XVII CENTVRY FRANCESCO
FONTANA BVILT FOR POPE INNOCENZO XII A CVSTOM'S
HOVSE FOR OVERLAND TRADE, THE DOGANA DI TERRA, WITH
THE ENTRANCE AT RIGHT-ANGLES TO THE AXIS OF THE
REMAINS OF THE COLVMNS. IN 1870 THE BVILDING WAS
RENOVATED AND BECAME THE SEAT OF THE STOCK EXCHANGE
AND THE CHAMBER OF COMMERCE. IN 1925 THE BASEMENT
AND THE COLVMNS WERE EXCAVATED AND ISOLATED,
EMPHASIZING THE PRESENCE OF THE TEMPLE.

Signs for pedestrians: 71
over-design

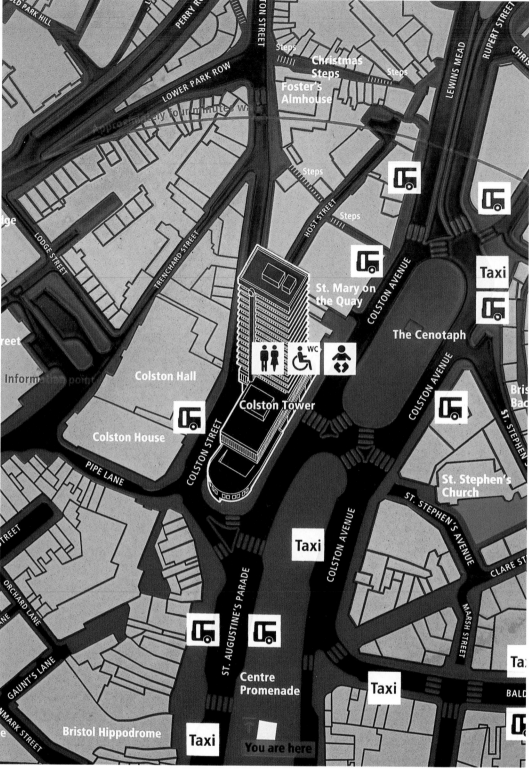

72 Signs for pedestrians: mapping urban spaces

A major problem with conventional maps is orientation. North is usually shown at the top but unless you happen to know which direction north actually is, such a map, when sited in a street, often leaves the user confused and disorientated: the map does not relate closely enough to its surroundings.

As described on page 26–7, 29 & 38–9, map-type signs for road networks are laid out as though 'straight ahead' is always at the top regardless of its true compass orientation. This approach has been followed in the new street maps for the city of Bristol designed by Meta Design, London in 1999.

This 'heads up' view is emphasized by showing the key buildings visible from each map as three-dimensional drawings. Although it means that no two maps are identical – the front and back of the same orientation sign shows two maps, each a different way up – their usefulness is immeasurably increased.

The maps are also noteworthy for being drawn from the outset with pedestrians of all ages in mind. They show what pedestrians need to know, such as the position of bus stops and zebra crossings, and each map is marked with concentric circles indicating 5 and 10 minutes' approximate walking distance.

73/3 COLLEGE GREEN, BRISTOL, UK 2002 (THE REVERSE OF 73/1)

73/4 NEAR TEMPLE MEADS STATION, BRISTOL, UK 2002

They are part of a new signing system which gives information only when necessary, and never shows more than five destinations in any direction.

74 Signs for travel networks: bus stops

The most common symbol for a bus stop shows a side elevation of a single-decker. This drawing seldom exists on its own, however, as most signs incorporate (at the very least) the numbers of buses serving that stop. Many signs also have provision for timetables and increasingly there is provision for features such as raised route numbers to help the visually impaired.

London bus stops, like those of many cities, do not use a depiction of a bus – not even the famous double-decker – but the symbol of the operating company, in this case the London Transport roundel (see also pages 80–1).

As with any standard, there are always examples which don't conform, but which are charming nonetheless.

75/4 BEDFORD PLACE, LONDON WC1, UK 2002

75/5 LOUTH, LINCOLNSHIRE, UK 1994

75/6 REYKJAVIK, ICELAND 2001

Signs for travel networks: 75
bus stops

76/3 & 4 OPORTO, PORTUGAL 2001

76/5 MÖNCKEBERG STRAßE, HAMBURG, GERMANY 2002

76/6 SHANGHAI, CHINA 2002

76 **Signs for travel networks: bus stops**

Bus stops can be considered pieces of street furniture. Generally, their position and the kinds of information they show are sufficient context for their purpose to be clearly understood even where language is a barrier and no symbol appears.

The amount of information each company chooses to provide about their various services can vary considerably. Of the stops shown here, only the second Copenhagen example on the previous page and those from Rome (77/2) and possibly Shanghai (76/6) would enable a first-time visitor to use a particular service without the need for some additional information.

Signs for travel networks: 77
bus stops

78 Railways: identifying stations

Within any travel network, lettering plays several key roles. It can be used alone, or with other visual elements as part of the identification of a company or service, but it can also serve to guide people around the stations themselves.

The examples shown here exhibit a variety of approaches which reflect the different periods of their design and perhaps some national design preferences.

The Paris Metro, like many early underground railways, took its name from the world's first: The Metropolitan Railway which opened between Baker Street and Farringdon Road in London in 1863. Early Parisian stations from the turn of the twentieth century (78/1 & 2) use both long and short versions of the name in the heavily stylized manner of the day.

Using a single letter as the symbol for a company is also a common device seen here in three countries. Britain's Tyne & Wear Metro uses station names designed by Kinneir Calvert (see also pages 24–31). Sadly, their proposal for freestanding sculptural forms outside each station was turned down. Instead, the company itself produced a series of altogether more mean-spirited designs (78/3). They seemed afraid that no-one would

Stephansplatz

S31 Harburg Rathaus

Dammtor – Hauptbahnhof

in 3 Min.

Gleis 2

MRT

Shelter

← 200m

ⓣ ÖSTERMALMSTORG

ANDREW
TO TRAINS ♿

TO BUSES →
JFK LIBRARY →
U - MASS →
BAYSIDE EXPO →
MT. VERNON ST. →
← COLUMBIA RD.

recognize that M meant Metro and repeated the word in another typeface. This is a not a worry for travellers in either Hamburg (79/1) or Stockholm (79/4) where letters make simple and clear statements in their respective city streetscapes.

The clarity of all these approaches might be compared to Singapore's Mass Rapid Transport (79/3) which uses its initials, a pictogram of a train and an additional logo in an unrelated and confusing manner.

The Subway in Boston is the world's second oldest underground, but its history is not at all evident from its station names and signing (79/5 & 6) which are clumsily set in all-capitals Helvetica with no space between characters or between lines. There is nothing welcoming or helpful here.

80 Railways: variety & identity, London's Underground

Even a short journey on the London Underground reveals a varied display of lettering, reflecting both its history and the changing tastes of lettering artists and designers.

While stations on the early lines – Metropolitan 1863; District 1868 (80/1 & 3); Northern (City branch) 1890; Central 1900 – each used a variety of approaches, the three lines which formed the 'Underground Group' – Northern (Charing Cross branch); Piccadilly; Bakerloo (all 1906–07) – used lettering in a more integrated and conspicuous manner. The stations, designed by Leslie Green, and later, Stanley Heaps, were all single storey and faced with ruby red faience blocks. Outside, lettering forms variations on a series of continuous friezes, typically in the 'curvilinear' style (80/2). At platform level, station names were glazed onto the tiled walls (80 /5). Although always five tiles high, they show a variety of interpretations of the same model.

The Underground's identity today comprises two, originally separate, elements, the roundel and the Johnston typeface. Originally solid, the roundel first appears on platforms from 1908 and in publicity material from 1910. The mosaic version (81/3), by Harry Ford, shows an early use of the logo as

an architectural/lettering feature. Edward Johnston's typeface was commissioned by Frank Pick for the Underground Group in 1916. The proportions of its capitals were based on those of the Roman Trajan letter (see page 122).

By the early 1920s, the Johnston typeface was being used with the roundel which had assumed its current, hollow, form. Although it was also used for other applications it is perhaps best associated with the brick and concrete stations designed by Charles Holden from 1926 onwards (81/1).

New typesetting technologies in the 1970s forced London Transport to revise and digitize the typeface. Overseen by Banks & Miles, New Johnston was introduced from 1988 for all new signs and publicity (81/2).

Following the creation of the Greater London Authority in 1999, the use of New Johnston has been extended to all aspects of Transport for London's business.

Railways: variety & identity, 81
London's Underground

82 Railways: ambience & splendour

Railway companies have always promoted themselves through their architecture as much as through their general publicity material. Stations, particularly in large towns and cities, were and maybe still are thought of as gateways to far off places and are designed in a grand manner to reflect that fact.

Both the examples shown here well illustrate a holistic approach to station design where all the different elements such as basic lettering and architectural detailing have been considered together as one convincing statement.

At Oporto's Estação de São Bento of 1910, the lettering is understated, appearing in discreet panels on the ceiling and above the various doorways.

In Florence, at the Stazione di Santa Maria Novella, designed by Giovanni Michelucci in 1933, the lettering is one of the dominant features. In this key example of 'razionale italiano' architecture, the lettering is both functional – signing the various elements – and decorative, making full use of the play of light and materials (glass, brass and marble) to create a powerful statement.

Railways: 83
ambience & splendour

CHURSTON FOR BRIXHAM

PASSENGERS ARE REQUESTED TO CROSS THE LINE BY THE BRIDGE

84/3 NEWPORT, GWENT, WALES, UK 1998

84/4 EXETER ST DAVIDS, DEVON, UK 1999

84/5 & 6 EXETER ST DAVIDS, DEVON, UK 1999

WAY OUT AND TO PLATFORMS 1-2

TO PLATFORMS 3,4,5,6

84 **Railways:**
old-fashioned reliability

Railway companies have always recognized the value of publicity and the role that lettering plays within that.

The approach of the Victorian and Edwardians in signing their stations reflects the tastes of the day. While examples can still be found in many stations (84/5 & 6) the full effect is easier to appreciate on preserved steam railway lines (84/1 & 2 and 85/1–3).

The rugged letterforms of Clarendons, Egyptians and sans serifs lent themselves to industrial production as cast-iron signs (84/1 & 2), or individual cast letters screwed onto wooden supports (85/1–3). Moulds of letters could also be used to cast glazed terracotta blocks (84/5 & 6).

Attempts at a coordinated approach to visual identity did not occur until after the grouping of companies into 'the big four' in 1923. These were the Great Western, the London Midland & Scottish, the London North Eastern and the Southern. The Great Western Railway adopted a circular monogram from 1933 onwards which was used on everything from locomotives and rolling stock, to benches and station buildings (84/3 & 4).

86/3 ST PANCRAS, LONDON NW1, UK 1998 †

86 Railways: legibility, arrows and pictograms

Britain's railways were nationalized to form British Railways in 1948. In 1964 a new visual identity was announced and the company name changed to British Rail. The identity was designed by the Design Research Unit (DRU) but the Rail Alphabet and signs were by Kinneir Calvert.

The successful design of directional signs such as those found in stations requires the careful consideration of the visual relationship between lettering and arrows. In the original design (86/2 and the top 5 planks in 86/3) the arrows are blue and balance with the black type. In the lowest plank of 86/3 – a redesign from the late 1980s – both arrow and lettering are blue which causes the arrow to dominate due to its size. The same problem of balance occurs in 87/3 but in dark grey. This example also features pictograms without any meaningful visual relationship to any other aspect of the design.

And why doesn't the top line just say 4 to 15?

The 1993 Railway Act, and the privatization which ensued, has resulted in new sign systems which reinforce the identities of the individual train operating companies rather than the network as a whole. The new colours of white out of a

dark blue (87/1 & 2) may have
a certain contemporaneity about
them, but the lettering is smaller
than before, and as a result, not
as legible from as great a distance.
Station names on platforms are
also far too discreetly sized and on
poorly-lit stations at night they are
really difficult to read at all.

**Railways: legibility, 87
arrows and pictograms**

88 Airports

The basic signing needs of an airport are little different from a busy railway station and their role in conveying reassurance is identical.

At London's Stansted Airport, designed by Sir Norman Foster and opened in 1991, the initial signing scheme is integrated with the building structure (88/1). The size of these signs seems, however, to have been designed to allow for a greater appreciation of the architecture rather than to respond to the needs of passengers. The tidy-minded and everything-ranged-left approach does little to suggest that not all the items listed are actually to be found to your left. History has not been kind to the scheme because in Britain no space is left empty if it can generate revenue instead. The columns have now become advertising hoardings while a map has been added below the main sign as an afterthought.

New signs at the airport are situated on stand-alone columns and are in the standard BAA style. Only the size of type is in any way an improvement. Everything else seems ill-considered, if not plain ugly.

In most countries other than Britain, it is considered desirable that signs on major public transport networks should contain information in at least two languages. Many of these signs also contain pictograms, making their design a complex balancing act if clarity is to be achieved.

One approach used to differentiate between languages is colour, another is size of type. The signs from Kuala Lumpur (89/1 & 2) use both, and create a clear distinction found lacking, for example, in the treatment of the three languages as used in Helsinki (89/5 & 6). When the languages use different writing systems, as in Shanghai (89/3 & 4), the situation is much easier to resolve graphically.

The design management of the Kuala Lumpur examples, however, falls down in just about every other respect, with information illogically grouped and non-standard pictograms (eg station master, tickets).

The signs from Helsinki and Shanghai exhibit a much greater design awareness in separating the arrows, pictograms and lettering. Confusingly, however, the Helsinki sign does not use the common pictogram for exit (see 89/2) instead showing one which suggests 'baggage reclaim'.

Railways & airports: 89
multilingual signs

**90 Railways & airports:
multilingual signs**

Like the Helsinki examples on the previous page, all the signs on this spread show information in three languages combined with the use of directional arrows and pictograms.

In the French sign (90/1) a partial language hierarchy – home and abroad – is indicated by size, but no distinction is made between English and German. The alignment of the arrows is used to reinforce direction but the treatment of the pictograms and platform letters is fussy.

The three signs opposite combine all elements with far greater clarity. They are from Korea and are helped by the fact that each language – Han'gul, Chinese and English – uses a different writing system. While the underground sign (91/1) uses coloured panels to reinforce the various parts of the information, the airport signs rely on the difference between the writing system and the graphic device of an inverted T alone. In the lower example the only significant improvement would be to group the right destinations together and align the left destinations to the left with their arrows on that side also.

The pictograms on boxes in this example seem to work better than the French sign because they visually match two of the scripts and the general way the sign is laid out.

나가는 곳 Way Out 出 口

갈아타는 곳 Transfer 換 乘 방화·상일동·마전 Banghwa Sangil-dong Macheon ⑤

26-50 登机口·搭乘口 | 탑승구 Gates

12-25 登机口·搭乘口 | 탑승구 Gates

어린이놀이방 Children's Playroom

어린이놀이방 Children's Playroom

免税品引受 | 면세품인수 Duty free Pickup

税關返送品引渡場 | 세관반송품 인도장 Delivery Point of Deposited Goods

按摩室 | 마사지실 リフレッシュルーム | Massage Rm.

转机宾馆 | 환승호텔 Transit Hotel

대한항공라운지 Korean Air Lounges

아시아나항공라운지 Asiana Airlines Lounges

Note also that not everything is translated into Chinese and that 'Massage Rm' is translated into a fourth language, Japanese.

**Railways & airports:
multilingual signs**

Good signing inspires confidence
in an organization: a masterful
combination of English, Chinese
and Han'gul on the Korean
National Railroad.

Time   **Destination**   **Expected**

1st 1256 Manchester Pic   1256
olverhampton, Stafford, Stoke-on-Tr
3rd 1322 Portsmouth Hbr   1322
Time Now   11 13 39

DEPARTURES

Time	Destination	Plat	Expected
1100	Taunton	10	1119
1113	Weston-super-Mare	10	On Time
1114	Glasgow Central	7	On Time
1115	London Paddington	11	On Time
1118	Manchester Piccadilly	15	Delayed
1119	Cardiff Central	12	On Time
1122	Portsmouth Harbour	13	On Time
1127	Weston-super-Mare	15	On Time
1128	Oxford	13	On Time
1130	Avonmouth	1	On Time

ARRIVALS

Time	Origin	Plat	Expected
1053	Weymouth	10	1114
1055	London Paddington	15	Arrived
1105	Gloucester	10	Arrived
1105	Bicester Town	13	Arrived
1109	York	9	Arrived
1110	Penzance	15	Delayed
1111	Penzance	7	1114
1118	Cardiff Central	13	On Time
	London Paddington	11	1143

Meads. Try the City Link bus 160 to the bla...

Time 16:20 Plat

BIRMINGHAM

Calling at
BANBURY
LEAMINGTON SPA
WARWICK
WARWICK PARKWAY
Dorridge
Solihull
BIRMINGHAM SNOW HILL

Front Train
CLUBMAN

Time 16:23 Plat 4

...N RISBOROUGH

Calling at
Wembley Stadium
South Ruislip
Denham
Gerrards Cross
Seer Green & Jordans
Beaconsfield
HIGH WYCOMBE
PRINCES RISBOROUGH

Front 2 Coaches

Lähtevä liikenne
Avgående trafik
Departures

			29	VIIMEINEN KUTSU
			29	VIIMEINEN KUTSU
07:35	AY651	Oslo	19A	VIIMEINEN KUTSU
07:35	BA6071	Oslo	22	VIIMEINEN KUTSU
07:35	AY661	Copenhagen	22	VIIMEINEN KUTSU
07:35	AY703	Düsseldorf	22	VIIMEINEN KUTSU
07:35	BA6019	Düsseldorf	25	VIIMEINEN KUTSU
07:35	DI4881	Düsseldorf	25	VIIMEINEN KUTSU
07:35	AY811	Brussels	30	VIIMEINEN KUTSU
07:35	SN533Z	Brussels	20C	VIIMEINEN KUTSU
07:35	AY861	Zurich	20C	VIIMEINEN KUTSU
7:35	AY871	Paris	20C	VIIMEINEN KUTSU
7:35	AA6183	Paris		

In addition to directional signs, passengers also need to be kept informed about service departure and arrival times and of any delays or changes to the service.

In the past such information would be given either by display units with interchangeable strips (which changed with a gentle, cascading clattering sound), or by making a sign large enough to contain every eventuality and illuminating the appropriate panels when necessary. However seductive such units were, they could only ever give predetermined information and needed the back-up of loudspeaker announcements.

The standard way of giving both routine and changeable information of this kind is now by using dot matrix (or similar) displays linked to a central information centre. Their advantage lies in the flexibility of the information offered.

Although the legibility of the letters themselves is compromised by the restrictions of a 7 x 5 grid or standardized elements, this can to a degree be mitigated against by the careful use of interlinear space, as in the example from Helsinki (93/3).

Railways & airports: 93
keeping up to date

Naming places and defining spaces

... architectural lettering cannot be reduced to function in the sense of legibility. Its function is to convey an impression, as well as to spell out words; also it is part of a whole, and must be related to the function and design of that whole. Gray 1960, p.39

In addition to directing and instructing us in our wayfinding, public lettering can contribute to the way we identify, and to some degree, respond to the places and spaces we visit. It is this idea of lettering as it relates to a sense of place which provides the theme for the remainder of the book. Here, our consideration of the ends to which lettering can be directed and the formal results achievable broadens considerably. The emphasis on standardization and uniformity demanded of many of the signs and sign systems already seen is replaced by a far greater concern with site specificity and individuality of expression. Of course, there are areas of overlap and while helpful, the key organizational themes of 'signing the way' and 'naming and defining' are not mutually exclusive. Modularity and manufacture then still have a part to play, yet, the rigidity of duplicable and ready-spaced typeforms, upon which so many of the sign systems we have hitherto discussed depend for their successful and consistent execution and implementation, is here somewhat overshadowed by the responsive potentiality of the discipline of lettering.

154/3

Lettering is concerned with how letterforms are both created and utilized. Both activities generally demonstrate a concern with formal flexibility that differs from the flexibility inherent in most types: within a single example of lettering, individual letterforms may be repeated or distinct, and their spatial relationships to other characters may vary according to context. It is this essential awareness of the context and the methods of production of a given piece of lettering which is exploited by the letterer. How much this is exploited varies hugely. At one extreme is the possibility for a highly creative and expressive intervention while at the other utility is a principle concern. It is the relative balance between these two essential elements of utility and personality which determines the scope of the field.*

What becomes clear when looking at the field of lettering is that the criteria for assessment cannot be limited to a consideration of the letterforms alone. It is a relationship of four main factors – letterform, placement or situation, scale and material – with the dominant influence varying from one example to the next. Situation, scale and material can all dictate the forms of the letters themselves giving them an unexpected beauty. Conversely, if ill-considered, these factors will diminish any value the letterforms may have in isolation. What is also true is that there is certainly no single style of letter which works for all occasions. Poor – or simply quite ordinary – letterforms can

* This discussion follows the ideas of Nicolete Gray, especially those expressed in her seminal book, *Lettering on buildings*, see the further reading section on page 186

also be transformed by scale, colour or situation. The considerable and hugely undervalued skill of the lettering artist lies in this ability to balance the impact of each of these factors in relation to the whole for each individual commission. Ironically, it is often the success of commissions sensibly and sensitively managed that renders such skill invisible. Unaware of the need for informed application and adjustment, the uninitiated wrongly assume that typeforms, as letters, can simply be transferred from one field into another.

Our examination of the way lettering practice can contribute to a sense of place is then necessarily based around these two primary and broad considerations of function and execution. The structure we have used to further subdivide the subject is then a compromise, and perhaps while more intuitive than strictly rational, it seemed helpful as an aid to focussing discussion. It balances a consideration of the more specific functions of lettering as it relates to the broader ideas of naming and defining – such as its role in identifying, enlivening and recording – with a consideration of the circumstances and the kinds of sites, architectural and otherwise, where such lettering is found.

Identifying locations

Naming and the use of lettering to identify specific locations are an essential part of negotiating our public environment. Some of the more pragmatic issues relating to this use of lettering have already been addressed in the previous section of the book, as signing and naming are in many circumstances two aspects of the same activity. But our sense of place is not just about a pragmatic awareness of our spatial orientation. What we find is that more than just providing a literal identification of location, the essential dynamic between utility and expression allows for lettering to say something more about the spaces and places around us.

111/4

If we take the example of street naming, this task may appear to be dominated by utilitarian concerns. Certainly, in many of the more recent approaches the emphasis placed upon non-site specificity and the use of typeforms ties in very closely with the strategies advocated for signing rather than with the idea of expression.

To take practical concerns first: we need to read at a range of speeds, as passengers or drivers of vehicles, as cyclists or as pedestrians. This requires lettering or type which addresses the same set of concerns as for signs: size, colour, contrast and use of space. And like signs, a consistency of positioning is crucial – a street name, however glorious, is of no use whatsoever in the wrong place. But, while functional, the way such a scheme is designed will have an element of personality and this personality will contribute to a sense of place.

The definition of a sense of place through the way the local streets are named is nothing new. It's just that now, this is perhaps a little more contrived than it has been in the past. Many local traditions exist whereby street names are not merely carriers of a corporate identity, but where it is the lettering and materials themselves which generate the sense of identity. Examples of this balance of letterform and material combining to provide a very particular flavour of place are the painted signs of Venice or the carved signs in travertine marble in Rome (Italy) or sandstone in Bath (UK). In other instances, the expressive

108/1

element of lettering is given a still freer rein and the name and the architecture are inextricably linked (*eg* Chester Terrace, London).

The expressive capabilities of lettering for street names are not, however, limited to the use of hand techniques or the highly individual commission, as local character can equally be created using manufactured elements. As the need for mass production grew, the use of hand techniques such as painting and carving gave way to industrial processes such as casting or an increased reliance upon a modular means of generating signs. If well-managed the visual interest of such examples is no less diminished for their industrial element, and good examples can be found in Britain (cast iron), France (enamelled steel) and Spain (ceramic tiles), among other places.

108/6

The fact that so many of the older signs are still around is a testament to the civic investment made by earlier generations, to the practicality of their designs and to the quality of the materials used in their manufacture. Today, in our more identity-conscious world, schemes are often introduced purely for the sake of reinforcing familiarity with the apparatus of local government. That some schemes, such as the one for the City of Westminster from the late 1960s, happen to be exemplary designs should not blind us to the fact that they shamelessly and needlessly replace perfectly usable older models and can be seen as a kind of civic cleansing.

110/5

Resistance to such a clumsily dogmatic approach is, though, reassuringly in evidence, if not directly in the field of street naming then certainly in the way many villages are named. In the UK, standard signs are part of the general road sign regulations. Despite this, in many localities, craft-based traditions still flourish and many communities have taken matters into their own hands in deciding how their village is presented. When travelling, such examples certainly compensate for the banality of standardization, which while helpful to the tourist, can, from the road, leave one place looking much the same as the next.

Identifying and enlivening buildings

Our consideration of the way lettering helps our negotiation of the public environment extends to the way it can be used to identify still more specific locations through the practice of naming buildings.* The naming of buildings generally accords to either one of two approaches. Architectural lettering describes lettering which is integral to an overall structure and which is conceived as part of that structure prior to construction. Fascia lettering strictly describes lettering whereby allowance is made in a building for subsequent naming by sequential owners, but is more loosely used here to describe almost any other kind of temporary lettering applied to a building.

120/3

136/6

* The term building is here used fairly broadly and should be understood as including a range of architectural structures such as bridges.

For the purposes of this book we are most interested in architectural lettering. The sheer inventiveness which results from the consideration of lettering and building together is of instant appeal. Beyond that, the fact that the lettering is conceived as a part of an architectural whole from the outset opens up a broader consideration of the more physical aspects of practice. The particular circumstances of a site, for example, the juxtapositions it may introduce or the materials it may demand have to be worked around. That more variables have to be balanced by the letterer makes for a more interesting proposition in terms of our intended exploration/unpacking of the mechanics of practice and the skills of those involved. It is the degree of permanence of much architectural lettering which makes it seem more important that it is got right, and so more important that we understand how it works.

When we start to look at the naming of buildings as it relates to architectural lettering we find the greatest legacy in terms of examples is to be found in our town centres: in the traditions of our civic buildings. It is a matter of public duty that the hospital, the police station, the town hall, the school and the library should announce their presence to us, the gravitas of an architectural approach befitting the civic importance of these various places. A closer examination of such lettering reveals, however, a variety of tone from the robustly straightforward to the out-and-out authoritarian, reminding us that, as with other examples of lettering which identifies, naming buildings is not just a pragmatic exercise. Rather it carries with it a promotional aspect and, in the case of civic buildings, a political dimension as governments – local and otherwise – make good use of this medium to reinforce a sense of civic identity.

This capacity for architectural lettering to give voice to a sense of civic identity was perhaps most magnificently exploited in ancient Rome. As the architects, artists and letterers of this early civilization explored the potential of the medium, great quantities of lettering were applied across a vast range of structures for a whole variety of purposes (see also the subsection about the role of lettering to record), not least of which was the basic celebration of what was then still a new alphabet. Still impressive, even in ruins, the original effect at the time must have been truly remarkable. The potential properties of architectural lettering as an instrument of propaganda were not lost to ancient history, being exploited by the church throughout the succeeding centuries and totalitarian regimes in the twentieth century.

Of course, the use of architectural lettering to identify extends beyond the civic sphere, to both our more commercial and domestic spaces. Lettering of commercial premises will often respond to the function of a building, be it a theatre clad in exuberant letterforms or a dairy suggestive of a rural idyll. Some of the most interesting urban lettering juxtapositions occur when the functions of buildings change while the original lettering remains. In commercial terms, the architectural presence of the name of a business also offers a certain sense of robustness and implies something about the longer-term ambitions of the owner. Again, beyond the functions of identification and distinction from competing businesses, the opportunities for self-promotion have not been missed. The naming of industrial buildings in the nineteenth century was, for example, in large part about the announcement of the new-found social status and wealth of their owners. On a more domestic level, traditions in the architectural naming of houses, though rarer, do exist. More common is the detailing of house numbers which, although a minor factor of an overall site, is, when well managed, satisfying in the way that attention to detail often is.

Such enjoyment is a large part of what lettering is all about, whatever the scale. As used architecturally, either internally or externally, it can serve to enliven the buildings around us. In the examples with which we have thus far

132/3

121/2

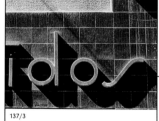

137/3

been concerned, this function of enlivening has generally been secondary, the happy result of a naming commission well-managed in terms of its relationship to the whole space in the hands of the letterer. But enlivening can also be the primary function. In some examples it seems that the actual name of a building is almost entirely incidental to the overall effect, in others there is clearly no purpose to the presence of words other than entirely aesthetic reasons.

Often the choice of words introduces a narrative element. Ecclesiastical spaces, for example, will often make use of extracts from religious texts. Context varies, though. Dwellings both grand and humble have, through the introduction of a poetic element, been visually dedicated to the celebration of language itself. With utilitarian considerations at a minimum, the potential for exuberance is opened up with results that can be simply breathtaking.

In spite of the essential dynamic of utility and creativity which can generate an infinite range of formal invention in lettering, it is clear that established orthodoxies can dictate. Letterforms have, in many cases, come to have quite specific associations of usage. The Roman inscriptional square capital, for example, is fairly well entrenched in more 'classical' traditions, but when used outside of these it has been criticized for its unforgiving nature: it can appear pretentious. Vernacular traditions have emerged, perhaps as a way of finding alternative voices to the classical idiom, but these too have had a similarly cohesive effect on practice.

Local vernacular lettering traditions have at various points in time and place been so strong as to have informed type design practice; in Britain, a form which can be called 'the English letter'* was used from the seventeenth to the nineteenth centuries and became the foundation for slab serifs of both the Egyptian and Clarendon variety. In America, a national association is favoured with the grotesque sans serif while a looser (sexy perhaps?) sans serif style is apparent in France, Spain and Portugal, distinguished by its characteristic sleepy 'siesta s'. Patterns of practice can also be determined by materials, typically by what is local or widely available. But other factors can play a part. Given the limited hours of daylight in Scandinavian countries perhaps it is no coincidence that a high proportion of fascia lettering uses neon.

The fact that many countries have obvious and extensive [rich] traditions in architectural lettering (Britain and Italy) or even fascia lettering (Spain and Portugal) is not to say, however, that these are areas of universal practice and in some countries such traditions are almost non-existent. And even where traditions have been strong, they can easily lose their way. To focus on Britain for a moment – it is perhaps easier to be critical of what we are most familiar with – the practice of architectural lettering is now very much diminished. A once vigorous vernacular was quashed by adherence to a revivalist orthodoxy in the early twentieth century. An emphasis then placed on particular models stifled creativity and led nowhere with the result that a flourishing and experimental tradition all but collapsed save for a few lone practitioners.

Yet there are broader issues underpinning the problems in architectural lettering today. Type has come to dominate. And where strong architectural traditions once fed typeforms, the influence is now the other way around

*First identified by James Mosley in 'English vernacular', *Motif* no.11, 1963/4, pp.3–55. Here we use Alan Bartram's simplified term, see *Lettering in architecture*, p.5.

– to the detriment of practice. Time and again we see typefaces produced in unsympathetic materials used in a public lettering context at sizes far larger than they were originally intended. Craft skills such as stone carving are seen less and scant regard is given to the humanizing quality lettering can bring to a sense of place through a simple combination of original letterforms carefully fashioned from quality materials. Yet, small businesses can't (or won't) afford much else than computer-cut plastic, and craft skills, when they are used, tend to be reserved for important formal situations.

A similar lack of vision has contributed to the influence of the corporate world on lettering practice where commercial buildings change hands so often that the architectural naming of property has become redundant. Instead, an unquestioning reliance is placed upon the paraphernalia of identity which is typically insensitive to the requirements of local context. Little consideration, for example, is given to the thought that what might work on a letterhead is by no means guaranteed to relate to a building, and is even less likely to do so if that building is not custom-made and comes with an architectural personality of its own. To take the retail environment as an example, nothing eradicates a sense of locality more than the consistent promotion of an identity. In Britain, perhaps more than in other countries, every town centre looks practically identical.

But there are have also been wider shifts in architectural practice which have contributed to the diminished role of architectural lettering. The greater homogeneity in previous architectural styles necessitated the naming of our buildings as a means of their individual distinction. Now, surrounded by the fallout of architectural postmodernism we find that many of the buildings have become personalities of the urban environment in their own right and have no need of further visual definition by means of lettering.

113/2

Postmodernism has resulted too in a new found interest in nostalgia, an unhealthy sentiment in maintaining vigour in practice. Aside from the contemporary, lettering in 'historically sensitive' districts has also suffered at the hands of heritage lobbyists resulting in what is at best sterile imitation and at worst bad history.

Enlivening spaces

If contemporary architectural practice ignores lettering, this has been to some degree compensated by an increase in public arts patronage. The increased interest from the art world in the possibilities of words in art continues the traditions of concrete poetry which have flourished since the 1960s.

The resonance words can have, especially when used at a large scale and in the public domain is celebrated in the earliest examples of the lettering of Rome already mentioned and is still very much part of lettering as it is used to enliven. Language though can be exclusive. As our populations become ever more mixed and multicultural, we may yet see practice diversify and a far more open approach to language emerge.

The joy for the letterer is the freedom of approach that can be exercised. The lettering does not have to fulfil a utilitarian role but can simply exist as art and contribute to the quality of a space. Poetic texts have, in the hands of letterers, visually transformed once plain community areas. Other community-based

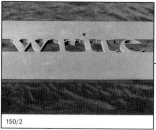

150/2

158/4

projects have seen the involvement of designers, usually through the out-working of projects managed in a more environmental way than is generally the norm. Pavements, walks and the various civic spaces through which people pass have all provided particular areas of focus for projects.

As a relatively new area, however, there is far less ground to cover than for other areas of public lettering, and like architectural lettering, this aspect of practice is not universal. Some national distinctions are also beginning to emerge, and this may be for practical reasons as much as anything else. In a country such as the Netherlands, a percentage of the budget allocated for new building projects is designated for art projects, and so funding opportunities are greater. But it is also a wider cultural issue. Some of the most significant work we cover is from Barcelona, the city which introduced us to a considera-tion of this whole dimension of lettering practice and a city which clearly has a very healthy tradition of public art patronage. We can learn much from the work of two sculptors in particular, Josep María Subirachs and Joan Brossa. Their pieces exhibit a freedom of form and application quite different from any of the other work we have shown, and yet never become so indulgent that they fail to make positive contributions to the surrounding architecture, townscape and the broader study of lettering itself.

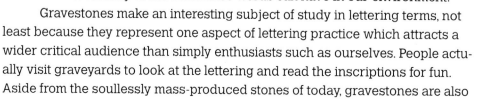

160/4

Recording

Lettering has long served as a means of recording for the benefit of a wider audience, and for posterity, the scope of human achievement from the triumphant to the trivial. And while this section cannot hope to be comprehensive in terms of the material it covers, it will attempt to represent something of the diversity of circumstances under which memorial lettering is commissioned and the diversity of practice which can result.

Triumphalism is perhaps best represented by the so-called triumphal arches of the Romans, dedicated to battle victories in the cause of their empire or simple vainglory. Triumphalism is equally the determining factor in record-ing the achievements in the name of later empires, the victory bridge to the Battle of Waterloo in Betwys-y-coed, North Wales being an eccentric but wholeheartedly pleasing such nineteenth-century example.

In the century after that which witnessed the two most devastating wars in living history, the desire to record battle is no less diminished, but the ration-ale is less partial in spirit. Lettering no longer serves to publicly declare a victor, rather it becomes the simple instrument by which the presence (often more accurately the absence) of hundreds of thousands of individuals is recorded. In these memorial records of war and atrocity the great power in the simple ex-pression of an individual name is perhaps felt only by those who have lost loved ones, but the power of the expression of names or numbers *en masse* is intense and further testimony to the resonance words can have in our environment.

170/4

Gravestones make an interesting subject of study in lettering terms, not least because they represent one aspect of lettering practice which attracts a wider critical audience than simply enthusiasts such as ourselves. People actu-ally visit graveyards to look at the lettering and read the inscriptions for fun. Aside from the soullessly mass-produced stones of today, gravestones are also

179/6

interesting because the letterforms used are among some of the most immediate – many of the much older examples are intuitively cut and have quite a story to tell concerning vernacular practice. Yet, that is a subject for the specialist book. Here, our representation of gravestones is small and is focussed upon more recent and highly individual examples or an unfamiliar choice of material.

And then to the other many lettering incidentals which surround us: the many plaques which record the historical fact or cultural significance of the places and spaces around us; the marks left by builders, architects and craftspeople proud of their work; the detailing added to a downpipe or some other such utilitarian part of a building to record a year; the manufacturer's name on a manhole cover to promote their trade. To this list of incidentals which record can be added those other lettering incidentals which, strictly speaking, fulfil other kinds of functions, but which are so similar in scale it is helpful to consider them altogether: the lettering clues which alert us to the presence of, among other things, gas pipes, telephone cables and water hydrants.

These individual elements may seem insignificant on their own, yet while small and typically undramatic in function they are often surprising in terms of how well designed and detailed they are. Collectively, it is the details such as these which determine the visual texture of our public environment and in doing so contribute much to our sense of place.

Possibilities

There is so much that is uninspiring and unsuccessful in lettering terms that it is all to easy too become used to bad practice and simply accept it. In the past there was certainly a greater variety of letterforms and materials used, but rather than wearing 'heritage-tinted' glasses and feeling nostalgic, we should look to them for inspiration and remind ourselves of the multitude of possibilities of both letterform and material. In the recent examples we have found – which do visually enrich our experience of letterforms and the environment – there is still much to catch the eye.

QUEENS - LANE

NICHOL-HILL

BANKS ST.

LINACRE ROAD, N.W. 2

CAT HILL A110

KING'S PARADE

104 Identifying locations: street names, individuality & standardization

Many of the individual signs by which we identify our streets are elements of wider sign systems. Such systems necessarily reflect a non-site-specific approach to design; each sign is required to function – be visible and clear to read at a variety of speeds – wherever it is placed.

While not responding directly to individual sites, however, a local system may well be able to take into account broader considerations of architectural style or widely-used building materials resulting in systems visually sympathetic to their context. As shown, colour can provide a useful tool for distinguishing signs from a background, with blue being especially successful against brick.

A visual sympathy between street names and a local area may also derive from using local manufacturers whose work is rooted in an appreciation of that locality. As the examples show, the visual resonance of such locally made signs is no less diminished for them having been industrially manufactured. The use of casting techniques (104/1, 2 & 4) and vitreous stove enamelling (104/3) certainly brings with them a degree of robustness which means that many older examples are still in use today.

Reflecting the twentieth century's trend towards the centralization and standardization of industrial manufacture generally, some attempts have been made to produce national (cheap) solutions. At one end of the spectrum are matter-of-fact signs using pre-1964 Department of Transport lettering (104/5) while at the other are letterforms designed by David Kindersley (104/6). Of these last two, 104/5 has a no-frills approach which seems to suit manufacture in pressed-steel, while Kindersley's letters, derived from carved Roman forms, seem far too civilized (not to mention cramped in the space) for that treatment.

In contrast to such lame attempts at uniformity, the gesture of the individual can seem all the more invigorating. One of the grandest of all such gestures is surely John Nash's wonderfully robust statement from his Chester Terrace development of c.1825.

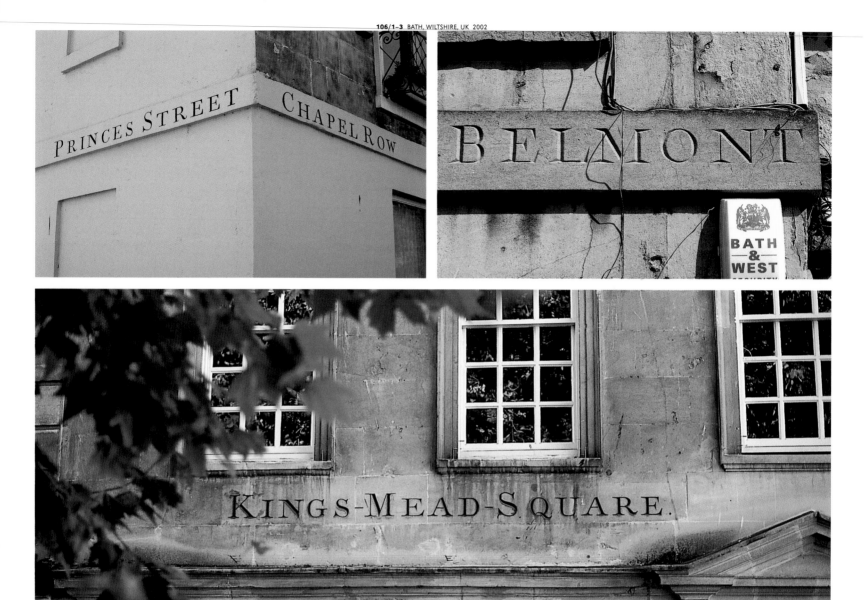

106 Street names: materials & letterforms

Nowhere in Britain is the visual sympathy between street names and local context more cohesively demonstrated than in the city of Bath. A combination of the city's scale, a certain homogeneity in architectural style and use of building materials as it developed in the eighteenth and nineteenth centuries have all allowed for a consistency of approach to this most basic civic orientation problem.

The street names are inscribed directly onto the buildings in letterforms contemporary with the style of architecture. The immediacy of this technique affords these signs an architectural sensitivity which is difficult to achieve with signs that are physically attached to a building. Even at the considerable scale required for ease of reading, the inscriptional names never seem visually invasive.

While consistent in approach, their execution is never pedantic. Letterforms do differ. Most typical is a square roman letter identified as 'the English letter' (see page 100) whose simple proportions compliment the straightforward robustness of the dominant Georgian style (106/1 & 3). In contrast, a later belt of terraced cottages on the outskirts of town have been appropriately identified with nineteenth-century

107/1–4 BATH, WILTSHIRE, UK 2002

107/5 BRISTOL, UK 2002

107/6 KENDAL, CUMBRIA, UK 1999

sans serif forms (107/3 & 4).
In some instances the differences
in letterforms are due to later
recutting. 106/2, for example,
is an altogether harsher form than
the simpler vernacular letter with
longer and much sharper triangular
serifs. Many early idiosyncrasies of
cutting do, though, still remain as is

illustrated by the deviation to
a sloped form in 107/1 and the
simple lack of surety of 107/2. Far
from detracting the eye, however,
the difference that such details
make to the overall visual texture of
the city only seems to add to one's
sense of the character of the place.
Though most cohesively demon-

strated in Bath, the benefits of this
approach to street naming have
been capitalized upon by a number
of other towns and cities (107/5 &
6), and in some cases very far afield
(see overleaf).

Street names: 107
materials & letterforms

108/3 OPORTO, PORTUGAL 2001

108/4 CARVOEIRO, ALGARVE, PORTUGAL 1996

108/5 & 6 LAS PALMAS, GRAN CANARIA, SPAIN 1999

108 **Street names:**
materials & letterforms

The use of particular materials provides cities and even countries much further afield with a certain visual identity and sense of place.

As in Bath, the street names of Rome are inscriptional (108/1 & 2), but are not cut directly into the buildings themselves, rather into marble slabs either set into walls or, less satisfactorily, mounted on posts. The lettering is consistent in its general approach across the city, but the borders are significantly more ornate on signs in more important locations.

Throughout Portugal tiles are commonly used in the manufacture of street names and the examples shown (108/3 & 4) originate from both the north and the south of the country. These typical tiled plaques are visually very much in keeping with the decorative tiled façades which are a common national architectural feature.

An altogether more typical approach to the use of tiles in street naming can be seen in the modular examples shown from Spain. While the flat glazed example (108/5) is representative of a method common in other countries including Britain, the relief-cast example (108/6) is far more unusual.

Elsewhere it is not so much the materials which distinguish

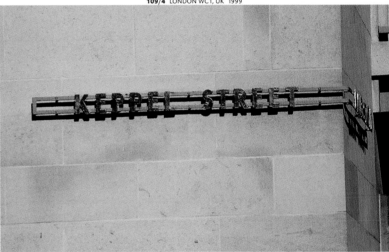

a particular approach to street naming, but the actual letterforms themselves. The squarely geometric style of sans serif letterform is certainly the defining feature of the street names in The Hague (109/1), while the ornate stencilled letterforms of 109/2 combine with a distinct shape of plaque to create a visual characteristic particular to Barcelona.

But while a given approach to materials or letterforms may well be relatively coherent across a city or even a country, there are always exceptions. Of the more local and individual examples, those shown here all illustrate the way colour and texture can be utilized to add to a given sign's sense of presence on the street. The results may be sophisticated (109/3 & 4) but even when less surely executed (109/5 & 6) the end product can often demonstrate the charm to be found in simplicity.

Street names: 109
materials & letterforms

110/3 & 4 REYKJAVIK, ICELAND 2001

110/5 COVENT GARDEN, LONDON WC2, UK 2002

110/6 SOUTHWARK, LONDON SE1, UK 2001

110 Street names: physical presence

In the majority of instances, systems for street naming simply involve signs which are applied to existing buildings or custom-made posts or structures.

As the signs are required to be clearly identifiable in spite of the variety of backgrounds upon which they might appear and the varying degrees of visual noise which might surround them, physical presence is an important design consideration.

This sense of presence is often achieved through the careful consideration of the sign in relief and, in particular, the treatment of surface. A widely applicable strategy, as shown in the examples here, is to be found in a simple attention to contouring and the use of materials, such as vitreous stove enamelling which catches the light.

The examples from Iceland also serve to show a recent trait of visual over-articulation in the kinds of signs used in different parts of the city (110/3 & 4). The linear blue enamelled signs are found widely throughout Reykjavik, whereas the red and supposedly heritage-friendly signs are found in areas designated as historically sensitive.

Among the best postwar British signs are those in the City of Westminster (110/5) designed by Chris Tinings at the DRU circa 1968.

The clear typographic arrangement uses Univers Bold Condensed on enamelled steel with a 25mm return. This gives these signs considerable physical presence. The more recent example from London (110/6) shows a reassuring restraint in promoting a particular area. In addition to its depth, it also illustrates the benefits of a border in distinguishing sign from background.

In many schemes a sense of physical presence is achieved through the use of custom-made posts or structures which can both impose and allow for a greater degree of control over where signs might be positioned and therefore distinguished.

Primary considerations in the design and manufacture of such posts and structures include detailing, overall shape and height.

Approaches to detailing can range from the ornamental and imposing (111/1) to the straight-forwardly plain (111/3). Again, as with most signing situations, it is simplicity which often works best (111/2 & 4). The post, fastening and economy of space and layout of the sign for Chiquella Lane is exemplary in its brutal efficiency.

**Street names: 111
physical presence**

GREENMARKETSQUARE
GROENTEMARKPLEIN

ASCAL SAN NIOCLÁS
NICHOLAS AVENUE

HING HON ROAD
道漢興

ΟΔΟΣ
ΦΙΛΙΠΠΟΥ
FILIPPOU

53 → 55

شارع أم الشيف
Umm Al-Sheif Rd

← القسائم 29- 3 PLOTS

Upp Cross St
克罗士街上段

CHINATOWN
牛车水

112 Street names: bilingual signs

The main problem of bilingual signs has been mentioned earlier (see pages 34–5 & 89–92) – the need to clearly differentiate between two languages.

As with the directional signs, colour is useful when two languages are written in the same writing systems, as can be seen in the example from Cape Town (112/1) where no attempt at distinguishing between English and Afrikaans has been made.

All the other signs have names written in two different alphabets or writing systems which tend to differentiate themselves more naturally. While the Irish example (112/2) commits basic typographic crimes – word spaces too large (a problem in 112/3 also) and leading too tight – the remainder are much clearer simply because of the difference in script.

Often, as part of some scheme of civic enhancement, or perhaps because administrative boundaries and names have changed, local authorities decide that an indiscriminate replacement or duplication of perfectly serviceable –and often quite beautiful – signs is in order. One has to ask 'Why?'

In the EUR suburb of Rome, cheap steel poles sit alongside carved marble (113/1).

In London's West End, a sign easily readable across the street (see also 109/3 for size) is taken down and replaced by a twee 'heritage' label (113/2) which is only legible at half the distance.

In the City of London, a serviceable old sign is joined by a corporate model of 1988 vintage. The coat of arms on the new sign may be heraldically correct but is quite overbearing and the frame swamps everything, the simple use of the crest on the older sign is far better.

Street names: 113
a dog marking its territory

114/4 B556, HARPER LANE, HERTFORDSHIRE, UK 2002

114/5 A1081, HARPENDEN, HERTFORDSHIRE, UK 2002

114/6 PIAZZA DELLE CINQUE LUNE, ROME, ITALY 2002

114 Boundary markers

Related to signs for streets and signs for places are boundary markers, which can denote any level of administrative area from parish to country.

Their form varies considerably and shown here are examples from Rome (114/6) which match the city's street names (see page 108), and from Cumbria (114/2 & 3) which match the milestones to be found there (see page 18).

Like milestones, the size and situation of these boundary markers makes them easy to miss when travelling on roads, also many old markers remain indicating boundaries or places which no longer exist.

114/2 indicates Westmorland, a county which ceased to exist in 1974. 114/1 stands at the original meeting point of Cumberland, Lancashire and Westmorland, while it is now quite firmly in Cumbria.

115/3 & 4 VENDÉE, FRANCE 2001

115/5 LINCOLNSHIRE, UK 2001

115/6 BEDFORDSHIRE, UK 2001

Grindavík

D 754
COMMEQUIERS

D 754
COMMEQUIERS

SUTTON BRIDGE 3 M
LONG SUTTON
FLEET HARGATE 2 M

CAMPTON

In addition to directional and other signs, there is also the need to announce towns and villages. Sometimes this announcement sign is paired with a departure sign, as shown here (115/1–4).

Signs erected by the authorities tend towards uniformity, although the 1931/44 British versions were more helpful than most in their inclusion of distances to the two next destinations along a particular road (115/5). Note also in this example, reflectors in the letters which have since been painted out.

In addition to official signs there is considerable tolerance of local initiatives. 115/6 shows a variant of a 1951 Festival of Britain sign and shows how a simple change of shape can give a more welcoming aspect to the sign, while its situation and upkeep are an indication of civic pride.

Names for towns and 115
villages: the official and
the home-made

116 **Names for towns and villages: the official and the home-made**

Many local signs are not strictly functional in that they are often sited near the centre of a village rather than at its approach, but they have different goals. The official sign is about legislation, the local sign is about life, history and pride. The pair of signs from Northaw serves to illustrate the difference. By combining a speed restriction with the name, the official version suggests that the village is little more than a hindrance to traffic, its lower message is a sad indictment of driver standards and attitudes. The local sign says 'we live here' and 'we made this' which are far worthier sentiments.

Such home-made signs occur widely, but despite increasing car usage they are seen by less people because roads tend to bypass village and town centres. Most of these signs are made from carved and painted wood or wrought iron. They celebrate local history, forgotten heraldry and local scenes.

The King's Lynn sign (117/2 & 3) is the only surviving one of three different 'home-made' signs on the various approaches to the town. It depicts St Margaret on one side, and on the other side the architect and 1683 mayor of the town, Henry Bell, shown standing in front of the Custom House. It was designed and

WIGGENHALL ST GERMANS

KING'S LYNN

KING'S LYNN

HOLBEACH

SUTTON BRIDGE

LA TRINITÉ sur MER

carved by Harry Carter in 1959 who was also responsible for the signs at Babingley, West Newton, and Wiggenhall St Germans.

A careful inspection of other signs sometimes reveals who made them, and when. For example, Sutton Bridge, 'Plinth designed and erected by Victor Day & Louis Whitcombe. Sign designed & made by John Barker & Eric Tolliday, re-sited 1992'; Holbeach, 'Built and painted by Crispin Tylor from John Wolfenden's prize winning design 1984. Re-painted 1993 and 1998'.

The final example of a town name is from France and shows how it is possible for local author-ities to produce signs which can both look official and also respond to local situations. It says welcome, not the opposite.

Names for towns and villages: the official and the home-made 117

118 **Identifying and enlivening buildings: architectural (permanent) and fascia (temporary) lettering**

There are fundamental differences of purpose and approach between architectural and fascia lettering.

As a general rule, architectural lettering is conceived with, and is designed to last as long as the building. Neither the building nor the lettering should look quite right without the other.

The lettering on the Coliseum, home to the English National Opera company is a good example. Like all of the window surrounds and cornice work, it is formed from pale terracotta blocks which contrast well with the red brickwork. Those forming the letters are each about 52cm (19 in) high. Despite

the fact that the circular characters are only as high as the flat-topped ones and therefore appear smaller, this example is successful because of its sheer scale, the design of the letterforms – very typical of 1904 when the theatre was built – and their relationship to the architecture. Another factor in their success

is the unexpectedness of their position: one would expect effort and expense to be lavished on the front of the theatre, but this is the side wall facing a narrow alleyway.

Fascia lettering is applied to a building after construction and has a life independent of the building: shopfronts are perhaps the most

typical examples of this. When buildings are planned as shops, a defined place is usually assigned for the purpose (119/1 & 2) and this helps to lend a street or group of shops some unity.

Sometimes fascia displays spill over onto other parts of the building, ignoring the architecture. There are different degrees to which this happens, from the subtle (119/3) to the overbearing (119/5).

There are many different views about what is acceptable, and in which particular areas. In Athens in the run-up to the 2004 Olympic Games, large areas of the city have been cleansed of their fascia signing and advertising (119/6). Whatever the horrors of the old signs, such a radical removal has left a soulless streetscape.

**Identifying and enlivening 119
buildings: architectural
(permanent) and fascia
(temporary) lettering**

120 **Architectural lettering: considerations of letterform, position, scale and material**

The criteria for assessing architectural lettering cannot be limited to a consideration of the letterforms alone, as 120/1 & 2 show. Here fine letters following the Trajan Roman model are incised and painted in Portland stone, but they cannot compete with the monumental blandness of the wall.

Success depends on the relationship of four main factors – letterform, position, scale and material – with the dominant influence varying from one example to the next. In all the other examples on this spread the letterforms and architecture match each other perfectly in spirit and in execution.

At the London School of Hygiene & Tropical Medicine (120/3 & 4), the letters share a directness with the architecture, but their execution – in relief within a relief border – allows them to catch the light and, with the laurel wreaths, they form the most decorative element on the whole façade.

Both the Bank of Finsbury (120/5 & 6) and Saint Martin's Schools (121/1 & 2) have lettering which Bartram calls the 'English letter': robust, with even proportions for all the letters (unlike the Roman model), and a strong contrast between thick and thin strokes. At the bank the lettering runs in two

friezes created for that purpose. They are cast in stucco and were originally presumably painted or gilded for better effect.

The letters on Saint Martin's Schools are incised. The three lines make a good teaching aid, explaining precisely what good and bad architectural lettering is. The top line is well positioned but has weak letterforms, the date has good letters but is incredibly cramped. The middle line is near perfect: rich letterforms, well-spaced, and elegantly arranged in their setting.

122 Architectural lettering: Italy, from the Republic to the Renaissance

Widely recognized for their extensive and early contribution to the field of architectural lettering, the ancient Romans certainly established a precedent for a tradition of monumental inscription which continues today.

Letterforms were incorporated into a vast range of structures across Rome (and later the empire) from bridges to triumphal arches (see page 162), tombs and places of worship. In part this can be seen as a simple celebration of what was then still a new alphabet. Yet what is also clearly evident, even in the ruined structures remaining, is the remarkable potential of the medium of lettering as a tool for promoting civic identity.

The basic letterform employed can be broadly identified as a square Roman capital letter. That is to say, the widest letters are based on square proportions with the proportions of the others observing a loose set of geometrical derivations.

However, changing materials and sensibilities were to result in a huge degree of variation upon this basic formal theme which only becomes more evident as history progresses.

The inscription on the Ponte Fabricio (122/3), which announces the date of its construction, mostly illustrates a simple form of letter,

123/1 SANTA MARIA NOVELLA, FLORENCE, ITALY BEFORE 1991

123/2 PALAZZO DELLA CANCELLERIA, ROME, ITALY 2002

123/3 CHIESA NUOVA, ROME, ITALY 2002

123/4 SANT' IGNAZIO, ROME, ITALY 2002

123/5 & 6 BASILICA DI SAN PIETRO, ROME, ITALY 2002

in contrast to the more detailed forms – greatly helped by the later use of marble – on the inscription to Augustus' nephew, Lucius (122/1).

The lettering on the Pantheon (122/2) illustrates another common practice, that of infilling square-cut letters with bronze. The inscription dates from AD 120–5 but the letters

shown result from restoration work in the late nineteenth century.

This strong use of lettering across the frieze of a temple was later echoed and became the norm for lettering on the façades of palaces and churches from the Renaissance onwards. Still further reconsiderations of the basic

Roman letter followed with the sensitivity of Renaissance forms (123/1–3) and with the more standardized ideas of the Baroque (123 /4–6). Seen *in situ*, this letterform rarely fails to impress, even when, as in 123/4, it is (in terms of sense) applied almost in spite of the building itself.

Architectural lettering: 123
**Italy, from the Republic
to the Renaissance**

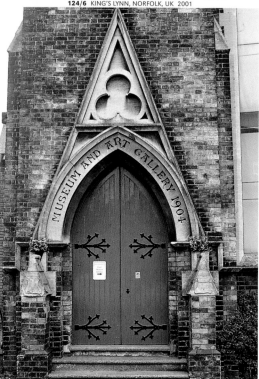

124   Architectural lettering: civic and industrial uses

In the increasingly urbanized society of post-industrial England, a new wave of building introduced new interpretations of the Roman precedent for using lettering as a vehicle for reinforcing civic identity.

What is remarkable about this particular 'English tradition' is its sheer formal inventiveness. The basic English roman letter (see also page 121) is exemplified in the robust square regularity and generous curves of the inscriptional letterforms of 124/4. Other key vernacular letterforms followed, with the Egyptian slab-serif (124/2) and the grotesque, a nineteenth-century idea of a sans serif (124/3 & 5) being especially successful architectural forms. These letters could be incised in traditional fashion, and could even be gilded should the purpose demand (124/5). This example alone is testimony to the superior visual resonance of an architectural letter solidly executed in sympathetic materials over a plastic corporate identity superficially applied. Yet, the simple strength of line of both Egyptians and grotesques was also well-suited to the newer but effective practice of using forms in relief (124/2 & 3).

Vernacular lettering traditions are not, however, exclusive to England. The process of industrialization

broadened the need to announce public buildings. 124/1, for example, shows a continental version of a vernacular sans serif on a public transport depot.

As architectural tastes in civic building changed, so these simpler vernacular forms were often forsaken for newer fashions (124/6).

This reminds us that, as with other examples of lettering which identify, naming buildings is about promotion just as much as pragmatism.

Being seen to be 'in vogue' certainly seems to characterize 125/2. Of the range of styles and materials illustrated, the sheer commitment and exhuberance of its faience work

make it one of the most enjoyable examples in the book.

The letters on the Oxo tower (125 /1) are similarly immodest. Here the *raison d'être* was to bypass a law preventing advertising on the riverfront. Recently refurbished, they are now illuminated at night.

Architectural lettering: 125
civic and industrial uses

126 **Architectural lettering: the grand gesture and humble details**

The grand gesture in architectural lettering terms is not restricted to civic and commercial buildings but has also been extended to domestic properties.

Of these, one of the grandest is Castle Ashby where a rare use of balustrade lettering – an extract from Psalm 127 – can be found surrounding the house (126/1 & 3). By virtue of the extent of this scheme and the solid simple form used – strong in line and minimal of serif – the different architectural styles of the building are seemingly bridged with ease.

The eccentricity of the original scheme was then exaggerated still further when, during the nineteenth century, a series of terraces was added to the house (126/2). The balustrade lettering was continued – though in a slightly more condensed form than on the house – with regimented walls of text which articulate the grounds and vistas with a series of pronouncements concerning the nature of life itself, and conclude with a dedication to the dead wife of the patron.

This is not to say, however, that architectural lettering has to be undertaken at a grand scale to be successful. Great visual satisfaction is to be found in the humbler use of letters as an aspect of detailing.

The following examples illustrate the way that careful consideration of scale, position, materials and letterforms can combine to create unique visual experiences within increasingly bland cityscapes.

Despite being 60cm (2 ft) high, the lettering (almost Gill Sans) which identifies Parson's Library (127/1 & 2) is the most reticent. Relief-carved and projecting about 2·5cm (1 in) from the wall itself, it forms an easily missed frieze just below parapet level.

As an example of thoroughness the Dairy Supply Company premises (127/3 & 4) are hard to beat. There are seven places on the two façades where the company name or initials appear. The lettering which is such an integral part of the original building has happily survived changes in ownership and has recently been refurbished.

The carved and raised name on Faraday House (127/5 & 6) shows one of the more playful approaches to our subject, some letters being reduced to abstraction making them legible as letters only when seen in the context of the rest. The letters are carved from the blocks making up the wall and, until 1995, were self-coloured. Unpainted, they were emphatically part of the wall, a fact since disguised by colour.

**Architectural lettering: 127
the grand gesture and
humble details**

128 Architectural lettering: success & failure

One of the mistakes made in architectural lettering today is the simple enlargement of typeforms in the false hope that scale alone can create the required impression.

Sir Norman Foster's transformation of the area encircling the former Reading Room at the British Museum exemplifies this. With its flat, slightly blue light and swimming pool acoustics, it feels as though you're walking through a computer-generated image. The drum of the Reading Room is surmounted by an inscription saying: THIS GREAT COURT CELEBRATING THE NEW MILLENNIUM IS DEDICATED TO HER MAJESTY QUEEN ELIZABETH II AD 2000.

Square-cut by machine in Rotis (to the architect's instructions) it fails at several levels. The letterforms were never designed for use at this size and, without modification, look weak; the shallow cut is insufficient to attract daylight; and they are set too close to the lights to be visible when they are on.

Lower down on the 'drum' the sponsors' names were cut by Martin Cook, who was able to persuade the architect that a V-cut would attract the light more, and that modified letterforms would look far better than Rotis, while still matching the main inscription which had already been started.

The back of the Sainsbury Wing extension to the National Gallery (129/1) shows another example of an architect not fully understanding the difference between lettering and type. The font Times New Roman was square-cut in sizes which bear no relationship to the sense of the words themselves.

Happily, the external lettering at the front of the building (129/2) was more sensitively managed. The stone-cutter Michael Harvey used a deep V-cut in his own interpretation of an English roman letterform. Harvey also carved the magnificent frieze of artists' names alongside the staircase inside the gallery.

At Olympia (129/3) muscular letters reflect the masculinity of the architecture. As with Faraday House (see page 127) this has suffered by being painted (black, in 1975) but has since been restored to something like its original condition and has regained much of its glorious sculptural effect.

Architectural lettering: 129
success & failure

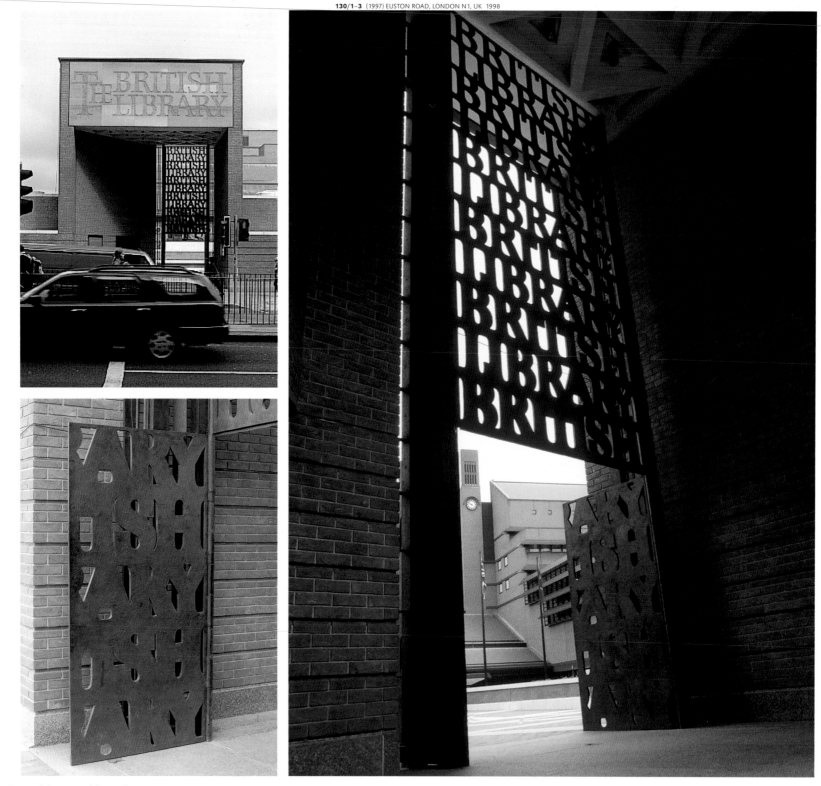

130 Architectural lettering: success & failure, the British Library

The British Library, designed by Colin St John Wilson, sits back from the road and is approached through the dramatic gates and across an enclosed garden.

The large lintel of the gatehouse features carved, raised letters on red sandstone. The work of David Kindersley's workshop, its individual letters and words are well formed, but the composition as a whole is fatally flawed because the over-large definite article dominates quite unnecessarily.

However, below, the gates themselves – cut out of heavy sheet steel – are much more successful: they do not contain lettering, they are lettering. BRITISH LIBRARY is repeated eight times and progresses in weight from 'light' to 'ultra black'.

131/3 *MON.TO F. MACIÀ (1991, DETAIL), PL. DE CATALUNYA, BARCELONA, SPAIN 2002*

Josep María Subirachs, born in Barcelona in 1927, was apprenticed as a sculptor in the studio of Enrico Casanovas, and sculpture has thus remained central to his working life. Through the 1960s and 1970s he became the city's best known, and most commissioned, sculptor working in a variety of ways – relief and three-dimensional carving, concrete and bronze casting – and for both civic and business clients.

Letterforms have appeared in many of his works, the earliest example being the mural for the Faculty of Law (131/1: a collaboration with Antonio Cumella) where Roman numerals simply suggest the ten commandments: three for God and seven for man.

A much later sculpture, the *Monument to Francesc Macià* (131 /3), shows another approach with lettering used in the manner of a caption both on the side of the bronze as well as on the back of the huge stone abstraction behind.

The Argos Publishers' building (131/3) shows Subirachs' interest in casting and the use of positive and negative forms. Unfortunately, a change in the building's ownership has led to the panels at the lower levels being destroyed at what must have been considerable expense.

Architectural lettering: 131
Josep María Subirachs
in Barcelona

132 **Architectural lettering: Josep María Subirachs, Barcelona New Town Hall and related work**

The New Town Hall is Subirachs' largest cast concrete work and with a number of other sculptures it represents a subtle, intelligent (and non-commissioned) civic branding.

In the design, Subirachs brings together elements and themes from several of his earlier works, and later goes on to 'quote' this work.

The complete mural is 2·5 x 45m (8ft 4in x 148ft) with the main design comprising the word 'Barcelona' and a map of the city. For the lettering, Subirachs experimented more with the forms themselves, abstracting them to lines and circular shapes and forcing the viewer to discover them so that at

first glance you miss the word 'Barcelona'. At the town hall the circles are filled with motifs relating to aspects of the city's history or to the construction of the building itself.

Like the lettering, the map (133 /2) is not immediately obvious. The city is turned 45° anticlockwise allowing the gridded street pattern

of the l'Eixample district to appear 'square' and the Barri Gotic district is simplified to a hexagon.

These two elements were reworked for two later commissions. At Sants railway station, the letterforms reappear with the background being made of casts of railway carriage wheels with

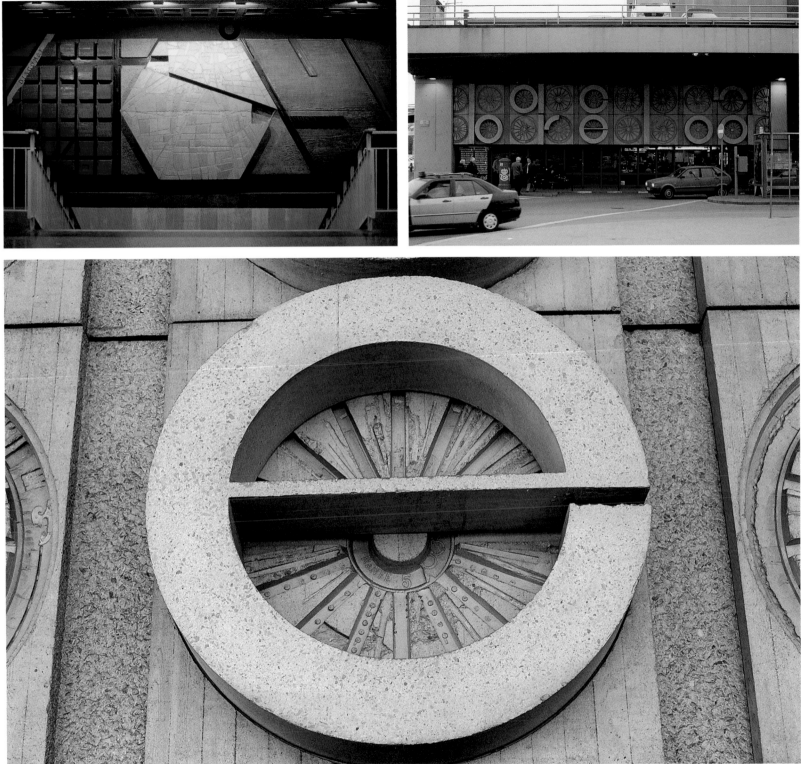

related items worked into them. The 'map' is reused as a mural in one of the subway entrances to Diagonal Metro station (133/1).

Architectural lettering: 133
Josep María Subirachs,
Barcelona New Town Hall
and related work

134 **Architectural lettering: Josep María Subirachs at Gaudí's Sagrada Familia**

The continuance of building works at the church of Sagrada Familia after Antonio Gaudí's death in 1926 has been a source of much heated debate in architectural circles, not least because Gaudí left no detailed drawings. Since the 1950s, the pace of work has increased and by the 1980s four new spires at the Passion end of the church were well on the way to completion.

Subirachs was commissioned to provide sculptures across the façade to illustrate the Passion narrative; to carve the four disciples on the towers named after them; and to design four pairs of bronze doors. For the duration of the commission (1987–2001), he lived and worked on the site.

While the outer pair of doors are mainly pictorial with short quotes from the Gospels, it is the two inner pairs which provide the main interest. from a lettering point of view. Each of the inner pairs contains an entire Passion narrative in Catalan (some 8,500 characters). The Saint Matthew door was installed in 1999, followed two years later by the Saint John door.

Each door began life as plaster casts of individual letters (135/1) which were then assembled into words on a grid, raised or set back

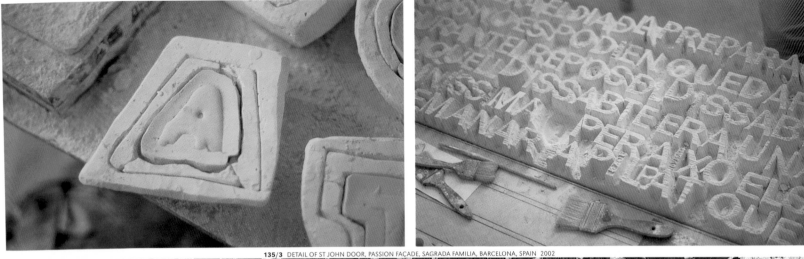

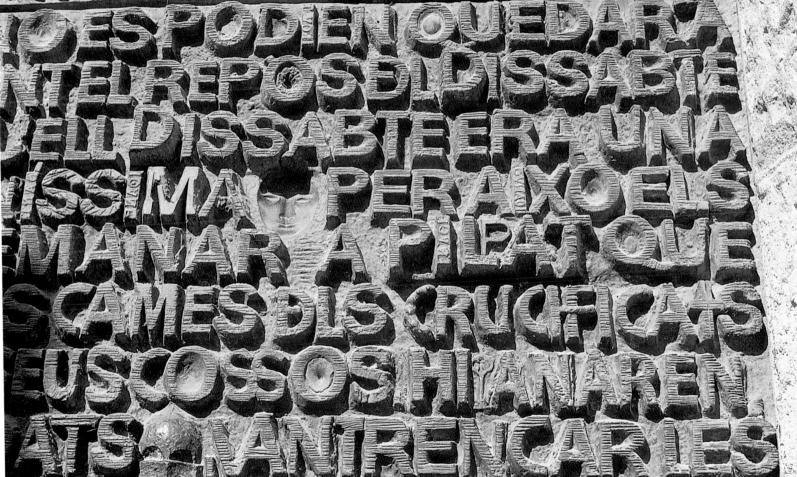

for emphasis or otherwise, and then worked on with various gravers (135/2). When a section 60 cm (2 ft) deep was completed it was assembled with other sections until the design was complete. From the casts a wax mould was made, and from this, the bronze doors were cast. 135/3 shows the completed section shown in 135/2. Subirachs checked each stage and made adjustments as necessary. After the doors were installed, certain words and phrases were selected for polishing (134/5).

Architectural lettering: 135
Josep María Subirachs
at Gaudí's Sagrada Familia

136/3 BARCELONA, SPAIN 1999

136/4 LAS RAMBLAS, BARCELONA, SPAIN 1999

136/5 MERCAT DE SANT JOSEP O DE LA BOQUERIA, BARCELONA, SPAIN 2002

136/6 OPPOSITE MERCADO DO BOLHÃO, OPORTO, PORTUGAL 2001

136 **Fascia lettering**

Because of the restrictions of their setting, fascia displays have to work hard to be noticed and at their best they show considerable verve in their combination of letterform and material, as can be seen both here and on the following pages.

Only one of the twelve examples on this spread is from Britain (137

/1), a country whose high streets have been blighted by chain stores with their corporate, one-size-fits-all approach to shopfront design. The remainder are from France, Portugal and Spain, countries where small businesses seem to thrive and sign-makers really know about letters, rather than simply knowing

how to connect a computer to a vinyl-cutting device.

Everything here has been drawn to suit the shape and size of the fascia, the material used, and many reflect the period of their creation.

The first six examples from Barcelona and Oporto (136/1–6) all make great use of mirrored and

reverse-gilded and printed glass. Both the thickness of the glass itself and the reflections achieved give the illusion of an even greater depth. In 136/4 this illusion is heightened by the *trompe-l'oeil* three-dimensional letterforms.

Despite the restrictions of a fascia, it is still possible to use real

three-dimensional letters as 137 /1–6 show. These are even more visually satisfying because of the play of light and shade which varies according to the time of day. Even plastic letters, if their forms and spacing are treated carefully, can look good, as 137/5 & 6 prove. Like 137/2 & 3, their forms exhibit a southern European approach to geometric sans serifs which can be seen also on pages 164–7. Among the typical features of this approach are exaggerated bowls to the letters *B*, *P* and *R*, and a low crossbar to *A*. On some Spanish examples – and 137/3 is the best we've seen – there is the distinctive 'siesta *S*'.

Fascia lettering 137

138 Materials & techniques: tiles, faience, mosaic and modular units

Ceramic mosaics have been a popular material for decorative purposes since Roman times. Their use is related to, and sometimes combined with, glazed tile work or moulded glazed terracotta blocks, known as faience (138/1–2).

There are two basic approaches to mosaic work proper, and both are shown on these pages. The first is to use broken or specially cut pieces in order to create any desired pattern, and thus preserve the integrity of the letterform (138/1–6 and 139/3 & 5).

The second is perhaps more interesting and involves using the material 'as bought', accepting its regularity and contorting the letter-form to that 'grid' This approach is similar to the overall effect which can be achieved using the units of regular building materials such as cobbles or bricks. 139/1, 2, 4 & 6 are all examples of this approach.

139/3 WALL OF HOTEL ABC, EGNATIA, THESSALONIKI, GREECE 2002

139/4 CERRADOS PIOS, CARVOEIRO, ALGARVE, PORTUGAL 1997

139/5 PARC GÜELL, BARCELONA, SPAIN 2002

139/6 UNDERFOOT AT ENTRANCE TO VALENCIA TOWN CENTRE, VALENCIA, CALIFORNIA, USA 1992

Materials & techniques: 139
tiles, faience, mosaic and
modular units

140/4 BADALONA, SPAIN 2000

140/5 PASSEIG DE JOAN BORBÓ, BARCELONA, SPAIN 2002

140 Materials & techniques: metal

It is easy to forget when viewing many examples of Roman lettering today, that metal was then an integral material with bronze letters cast to infill square-cut forms (see pages 122 & 162). The contrast between stone or marble and polished bronze must have added spectacularly to the overall effect.

Metal has since been made good use of for fascia lettering, but it continues to be used architecturally, albeit on a typically more modest scale than that of the Romans.

As a material it offers great flexibility in terms of scale, relief and the textures which can be generated. Certainly the Victorians were able to integrate often complex lettering schemes into their architectural ironwork, and the strength of the material is still put to good use in security grills, doors and gateways (see 140/1–3).

The strong use of positive and negative forms in these examples is carried through in other techniques and uses. 141/1 shows letterforms from a shop windowsill impressed into brass. It is probable that these forms would originally have been in-filled with coloured enamel. In contrast, 141/2 shows letterforms cast in relief in metal, again making good use of the potential strength of the medium for a shop threshold.

Stencil effects are also popular. 141/4 shows a simple but particularly effective use of cut-out steel and silhouette to announce a company's name down a small alley.

140/4 & 5 and 141/5 & 6 perfectly illustrate the way that an economic use of material and simple letterforms can, if carefully spaced away from a building or sign, take full advantage of changing light conditions. The letterforms both reflect light and cast an ever moving pattern of shadows. The overall visual effect somehow belies the simplicity of medium.

The examples shown here also demonstrate something of the range of letterforms which can be generated. Apart from 141/6 the examples here represent forms more individual in inspiration, with those created by Edward Wright in 1968 to identify the New Scotland Yard premises perhaps being the most famous.

Materials & techniques: 141
metal

142/3 HIGH STREET, WISBECH, CAMBRIDGESHIRE, UK 1998

142/4 NEW OXFORD STREET, LONDON WC1, UK 2002

142/5 BOSTON, MASSACHUSETTS, USA 1999

142/6 CARRER DELS TALLERS, BARCELONA, SPAIN 2002

142 Materials & techniques: ceramics, wood and paint

As previous examples have shown, ceramics have long provided another rich and flexible material source for use within lettering – their harmony with building materials making them especially suitable for use within architectural contexts. The garden balustrades at Castle Ashby (126/1–3) and the lettering on the London Coliseum (118/1–2) are both terracotta, while the façade of Edward Everard's (125/2) illustrates the glazing form known as faience, which not only improved resistance to pollution but also added colour. Cast ceramic tiled letters and plaster 'stock' letters (142/1) were also popular and came with the benefit of being ready-made. Plaster also offered the potential for colour as the layered example in 142/2 shows. The subtlety of colour and richness of lettering and pattern achieved here brings an unexpected richness to what is a dark and otherwise unremarkable section of street.

Stock letters were also mass-produced in wood. Incredibly flexible, these letterforms must also have been relatively cheap. Cut out in different cross-sections these letters were applied directly to the building itself (142/3) or to frames outside commercial premises (142 /4). In such cases, when painted,

SCALES WEIGHTS

WEIGHING MACHINE

319

321

ENTRÉE

HÔTEL

CIRCULATING LIBRARY
AND READING ROOM

these relief letters often blend so well with the fabric of the building that they blur the distinction between architectural and fascia lettering practice.

The versatility of wood also encourages an interesting, if not always successful, experimentation with letterforms (see 142/5 & 6).

Many commercial premises make good use of paint alone in the promotion of their trade. Old examples have proved surprisingly durable and many examples of the craft of the sign-writer remain on the walls of our cities (143/1–3) although the sign-writers themselves have all but disappeared.

143/4 shows a more contemporary use of paint on a building, albeit in a non-commercial setting. This is one of a series of texts painted on the side of a church as part of a local festival.

Materials & techniques: 143
ceramics, wood and paint

144/1 MONTSERRAT AERI, SPAIN 2002

144/2 MINNEAPOLIS, MINNESOTA, USA 2002

144/3 REYKJAVIK, ICELAND 2001

144/4 PARIS, FRANCE 2001

144/5 PLAÇA DE CATALUNYA, BARCELONA, SPAIN 1999 (SEE ALSO 145/1)

144/6 THE HAGUE, THE NETHERLANDS 1996

144 Materials & techniques: silhouette

The physicality of letterforms can be emphasized still further by their use in sharp relief or in silhouette.

In 144/1 the slightly awkward sans serif letters are not integrated with the architecture of the bridge or even centred upon it. Rather, their situation is a compromise between finding a convenient place to attach to the bridge structure and achieving maximum prominence for drivers on the valley road below. While lacking sophistication, these letters seem to work by virtue of the sheer surprise of finding them there in the first place. They certainly have an honesty found lacking in 144/2. Here, there is no correlation between façade and curvilinear letterform and the use of a framework, while common, can leave the letters floating somewhat unsatisfactorily.

A far greater sense of presence is achieved by adding bulk to the letterforms, either though material or section (144/3–6). And while the spacing of 144/3 could be better, even plastic can be seen to work through the use of a contrasting colour or material (144/4 & 6).

145/1 PLAÇA DE CATALUNYA, BARCELONA, SPAIN 1999 (SEE ALSO 144/5)

145/2 SORTEDAM DOSSERING, COPENHAGEN, DENMARK 1998

145/3 & 4 SVEAVÄGEN, STOCKHOLM, SWEDEN 1999

145/5 NEAR STUREPLAN, STOCKHOLM, SWEDEN 1999

145/6 SVEAVÄGEN, STOCKHOLM, SWEDEN 1999

Neon gives quite a different quality of light to a street scene than the cheaper contemporary alternative of backlit sheets of coloured perspex. Because making such signs requires hand skills – both to bend the heated glass tubes into shape and to create the support – there tends to be a greater awareness of letterforms by the signs' manu-facturers and, happily, more exploration of those forms.

In all the examples shown here, a balance has been kept between providing a sign which is as attrac-tive and clear by day as by night. In some of the signs the letters are trays in which the neon sits, in others the neon sits in front of the letters, appearing as an inline. Both methods are shown in the Conditori Café Madeleine (145/5).

146 Numbers

Numbers on buildings are an essential identifier of location. Aside from that functional requirement they can say much about the history of a building, the tastes and aspirations of the builder or owner or the period of construction.

Exhibiting a great variety of lettering styles and materials, most of the examples shown are small in scale, with the notable exception being the 2m (6ft) high brutally efficient DIN lettering painted onto the concrete walls of the U-Boat pens in St-Nazaire (146/3).

Numbers can also be afforded a prominence which makes them the defining feature of a given place or space. The cool linear numbers integrated into a steel gate by the architect David Wild (146/6) serve as an introduction to the unconventional architectural space beyond.

147/1 CARRER AMPLE, BARCELONA, SPAIN 1999

147/2 MARKET PLACE, KENDAL, UK 1999

147/3 SORTEDAM DOSSERING, COPENHAGEN, DENMARK 1998

147/4 OSTRANDVÄGEN, STOCKHOLM, SWEDEN 1999

147/5 CAMPS BAY, CAPE TOWN, SOUTH AFRICA 2002

147/6 LONDON EC2, UK 2001

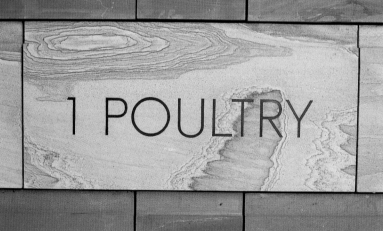

How many/Hours Bring full complete the Hour

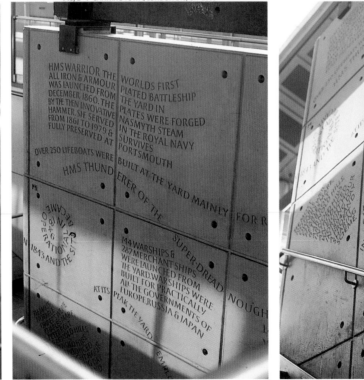

148 Enlivening spaces

Whatever the degree of visual experimentation employed in previous examples, they all have a primary functional role. While function is one aspect, letterforms can also be used in more subjective ways.

In many places local authorities, developers and other organizations have all been involved in commissioning art to enliven public spaces. As part of a continuing interest in lettering and words within the arts world, such commissions often feature lettering in a prominent way. In some projects it is the quality of lettering which creates the primary interest, in others it is the – often surprising – use of materials.

A detail of a collaborative design by Russell Coleman, Gordon Young and the Why Not Associates for the seaside resort of Morecambe is shown on page 2. Although *A flock of words* uses typefaces rather than lettering, an awareness of scale and materials ensures an accomplished result.

Opposite the Houses of Parliament is a sundial, a gift from Parliament to the Queen to celebrate her Golden Jubilee. Designed by Atelier Works with carving by Incisive Letterwork, the gnomon is formed only when a passer-by stops and stands at its centre (148/1). The text – from Shakespeare's

Henry VI, part III – is square-cut in pale granite so that the dirt which accumulates makes it more legible.

Richard Kindersley's lettering, carved into concrete at Canning Town station (149/1), responds to the difficulties of carving into that challenging material (concrete does not have the same predictable texture as stone). Encouraged by one of the architects, Jamie Troughton, to 'cover it with calligraphy' the text commemorates the previous use of the site as a ship building yard and the history of local football club West Ham United.

In London's Bankside area surrounding Tate Modern, several commissions featuring lettering have been installed in recent years. The architects Caruso St John were responsible for the district names which, although appearing in a consistent typeface, are executed in a variety of materials to suit different locations. (Other lettering from the area is shown on page 65.)

Enlivening spaces 149

150 **Enlivening spaces**

Working on a large scale is not essential to the success of these artistic interventions, rather, this lies in their appropriateness to the situation and the choice of materials.

Featuring words by Shakespeare, 150/1 forms part of the handrail alongside the River Thames close to the site of the Globe Theatre where many of his plays were first performed. Although the idea, setting and materials all work, the lettering (type) is something of a disappointment. Lacking the variety of material which makes the same designers' work at Morecambe successful (see page 2) it seems unsure whether to be playful or simple.

On a busy street corner, and standing as high as a person, a sculptural haiku (150/3) by Václav Vokolek uses steel in a more interesting way. Here the regularity of a standard typeface is offset by its far more inventive use of folds to create light and shadow which change throughout the day.

At Edward Square, north of Kings' Cross station, a much larger commission has brought together a specially written poem by Andrew Motion and lettering by Gary Breeze. Situated on one side of a low concrete retaining wall dividing a play area from a park, it is square-cut out of smooth cast concrete

exposing the textured and coloured aggregate beneath.

Like the *Visual-walkable-poem* (see pages 156–7) and *Groen* (see pages 160–1) this is a work which cannot be taken in at a glance but requires exploring on foot. The only quibble might be the fact that the wall has been painted with anti-graffiti paint which slightly lessens the appreciation of the materials.

The whole poem reads:
LIGHT LICKS ITS FINGER-TIPS
AND TURNS A PAGE OF EARTH
– THIS EARTH PACKED BENEATH US NOW:
IT GLEAMS OF ROMANS FACING BOADICEA,
FLOWS OVER CHARTISTS ON THEIR GREEN-SPRIGGED STAGE,

PICKS UP A RAILWAY-TREMOR IN
A TERRACE ROW,
THEN LEAPS TO HOLD A JUMP-JET
IN THIN AIR.
ALL DEAD, ALL LIVING, ALL A CONCRETE
SIGN OF FREEDOM LEARNING HOW TO
FIND ITS AIM:
TO PROVE OUR LIVES OUR OWN
– YOU'VE YOURS, I'VE MINE

– AND EACH ONE DIFFERENT BUT EACH
THE SAME.

Enlivening spaces 151

152 **Enlivening spaces:
Stephen Raw and
Ralph Beyer**

The particular significance of the idea of 'the Word' has driven strong traditions of lettering within ecclesiastical contexts with religious texts providing rich source material.

Featured here is lettering from both Coventry Cathedral and the parish church of St Francis in Wythenshawe, Manchester.

While forty years apart and very different in execution, these two projects are in fact related. Basil Spence was the architect of both churches and it was the lettering at Coventry which later prompted Stephen Raw to reconsider the role of media other than stone-carving in an ecclesiastical context.

In response, Raw embarked upon a six-month community arts project which led to the creation of an 8m² (26ft) mural (152/1). The prayer of St Francis of Assisi was chosen and local groups were galvanized into individually painting the 372 characters necessary, then brought together into the final composition

by Raw. The resulting installation is eclectic of style, gregarious in colour and magnificently vigorous in its interpretation of form. Sadly, the piece was only on display for one year.

The lettering at Coventry which so inspired Raw is similarly fresh and vigorous in approach. The new

cathedral (completed in 1962) included a large series of artistic commissions including lettering. Concerned that the lettering should all be undertaken by just one person, Spence approached the German sculptor and letter-cutter Ralph Beyer on the advice of Nikolaus Pevsner.

Of these projects, perhaps the best-known are 'The tablets of the Word' (153/2 and overleaf). The largest though, is a floor inscription which occupies the width of the nave at its west end (153/3–4). Anxious that the letter-forms should not become overly standardized, Beyer shaped the 67 characters individually before the forms were industrially cast in brass and set into the marble floor.

Each letter is about 1m (3ft) high and combined they read,

TO THE GLORY OF GOD †
THIS CATHEDRAL BURNT
NOVEMBER 14 AD 1940
IS NOW REBUILT † 1962

Enlivening spaces: 153
**Stephen Raw and
Ralph Beyer**

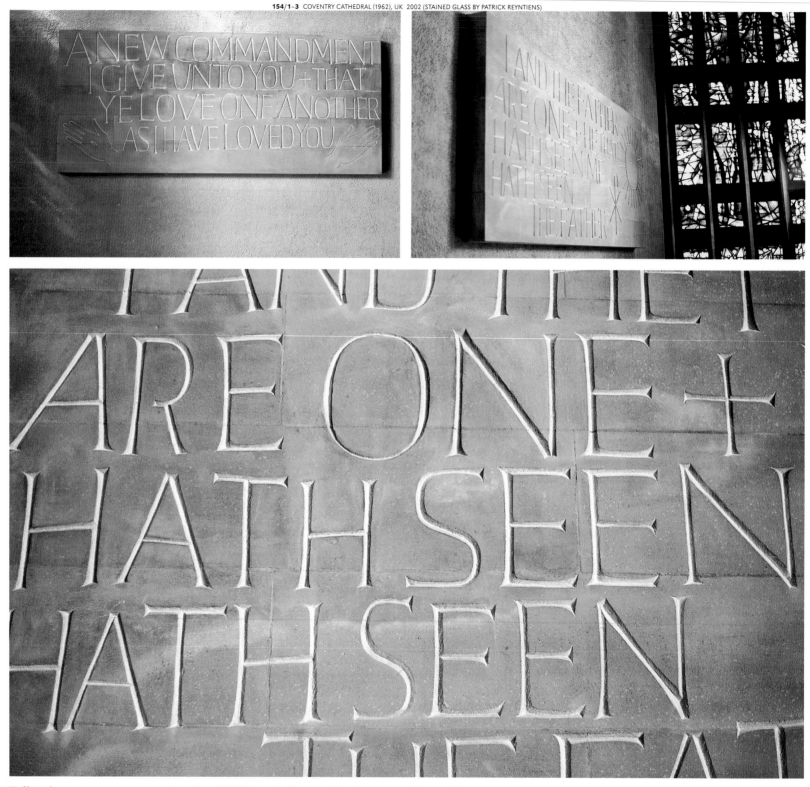

154 **Enlivening spaces: Ralph Beyer**

As early as 1955 discussions began between Spence and Beyer over the series of inscribed mural panels for the walls of the nave (154/2), later known as 'The tablets of the Word'.

Originally the idea had been to incorporate into the main body of the nave a series of themed worship spaces, each identifiable by a piece of sculpture. Yet, as the overall design evolved, the focus for these spaces shifted to the idea of 'the Word' and the representation of eight key New Testament texts which would address important aspects of Christian teaching.

Spence's original idea was for simple line incisions but as his knowledge of Beyer and his particular area of inscriptional expertise grew, so his understanding of the potential for this particular lettering project also grew. Encouraged by the architect, Beyer produced a series of original stone tablets (each *c.*14·6 x 2·1m [15 x 7 ft]) of lively forms which reinterpret the spirit of Early Christian inscriptions without being slavishly imitative. The letters, though highly individual, knit together in the creation of a rhythmic and richly patterned overarching sense of composition. As the light streams in from the stained glass windows the overall effect is only enhanced.

155/4–6 CHAPEL OF UNITY, COVENTRY CATHEDRAL (1962), MARBLE FLOOR BY EINAR FORSETH 2002

Beyer worked on two further commissions for lettering in the floor, though neither is as successful as that for the nave. A silver inlaid inscription runs across the floor of the Chapel of Christ the Servant. Simple enough, this must be considerably more striking when read as intended in the spartan atmosphere of the chapel uncluttered by temporary exhibitions. In that same chapel Beyer also carved the clumsier text for the altar step.

Not all the lettering at Coventry was by Beyer, however. A design for the inlaid marble floor of the Chapel of Unity includes an *A* and Ω and the symbols and names of the four Evangelists. This interesting and colourful design which embellishes Spence's original, much plainer, ideas for the floor was volunteered by the Swedish artist Einar Forseth and was undertaken as a bequest on behalf of the people of Sweden.

Enlivening spaces: 155
Ralph Beyer

156 **Artists & letters:
Joan Brossa,
Velòdrom d'Horta**

Joan Brossa (1919–99) was born in Barcelona and first started writing during the Spanish Civil War. From 1940 onwards he began experimenting with the form of his writing, creating what he called 'visual poetry'. Whatever else he later turned his attention to – theatre pieces, ballets, performance,

sculpture, magic, posters – poetry remained central to his work.

Official recognition of his work came relatively late in his life. In 1987 the (Socialist) city council (Ajuntament) made an agreement whereby his work was bequeathed to the City of Barcelona in return for a modest salary, a studio and

living accommodation. A new strand of work emerged at this time: the translation of several 'visual poems' into large-scale public sculptures. Although sited in public places around the city, the cost of their realization had to be met by him or other patrons. These letter-sculptures draw mainly on

ideas explored in the visual poems. With one exception, they are not architectural but environmental pieces whose form is dictated as much by the idea as the location.

The *Visual-walkable-poem in three parts* at the Velòdrom d'Horta is the earliest of the letter-sculptures. Commissioned by the

city council, it is also the largest. Part 1, 'Birth' is approached via steps and a footbridge, and comprises a 12 m (39 ft) high letter A. Beyond is part 2, 'The road: pauses and intonations', which is represented by punctuation marks lying at random intervals across a grassy slope. At the top of the slope are the broken remains of another letter A, part 3, 'Finale'.

It deserves to be much better known and visited, but its relative remoteness near the end of metro line doesn't help. However, its wooded parkland setting and the absence of crowds make this the most obviously poetic of his large-scale pieces. Because it is impossible to see the whole work from the start, and difficult to take it all in at the end; it demands the viewer's participation, you have to walk through it to understand it fully. The scale of each of the three parts and how they relate to the topography of the site is perfect.

Artists & letters: 157
Joan Brossa,
Velòdrom d'Horta

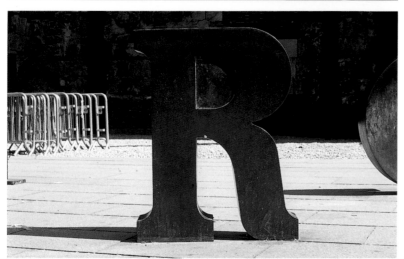

158 **Artists & letters:**
Joan Brossa,
***Barcino* and other works**

Of all Brossa's letter-sculptures, *Barcino* (Barcelona's Roman name) is the most public by virtue of its central location. Standing across a broad pedestrian square, the letters take on different forms suggesting the history and life of the city. The *B* and *R* are plain; the *A* is a pyramid and, as in many of his works, is the most distinctive letter; *C* and *O* represent the sun and moon; *I* suggests printing; and the single aluminium letter *N* is a bishop's mitre.

Like the Velòdrom poem, these are not related to one particular building but have to work in a space surrounded by very varied architecture. In the early morning and at night, they stand guard over the space, whereas during the day – especially a market day – they merge into the bustle.

In the suburb of Badalona, a printed visual poem *On es Bada l'ona* ('Where is Badalona?' or 'Where the wave is guarded') was later realized in three dimensions at two locations (159/1 & 2). One, on top of a school, where in certain light and cloud combinations, it appears to disappear into the sky; and the other cladding a radio mast beside one of the main roads north from Barcelona.

In many ways, these are the weakest of the letter-sculptures, one

159/4 & 5 *VISUAL POEM FOR A FAÇADE* (1993), BON PASTOR 5, BARCELONA, SPAIN 2001

being rather small and unrelated to the school, and the other not quite the right shape and size relative to the structure of the radio mast.

More architectural than *Barcino* and *On es Badalona* is the *Visual poem for a façade* (159/3 & 4) on the Col·legi d'Aparelladors i Arquitectes Tècnics de Barcelona where the letters needed for the name are arranged alphabetically on the façade, each letter in a different colour. Below them, running horizontally above the ground floor windows, they spell out the name. These plastic letters in the typeface Univers feel far more sophisticated than might be expected of the material. The fact that they project forward on pins creating shadows, and the random nature of the colours suggest the jollity of a toy shop, but the whole is a simple statement about process.

Artists & letters: 159
Joan Brossa,
***Barcino* and other works**

160   **Artists & letters:**
      Maarten de Reus, *Groen*
      in Carnisselande

In many countries large public building schemes must allocate a percentage of their budget to art. In the Netherlands, the city of Barendrecht, south of Rotterdam, has recently been building a new suburb called Carnisselande.

Its general artistic plan was known as *Elastic perspective* and was conceived by Albert Kliest and Joost van Hezewijk. It contained several 'dimensions' and in 1999, in a separate competition for the 'environmental' dimension, Maarten de Reus was commissioned to make *Groen* (*Green*) for the large roundabout at the entrance to the district. The open-ing took place in summer 2002 but it will take between 5 and 10 years for each 5m (13ft 3in) high letter to be covered in ivy (a local school of agriculture has adopted the project to take care of its maintenance).

De Reus, a sculptor, did not use an existing typeface but designed the letters as 'boxy, architectonic volumes'. *Groen* cannot be read from any one point but is a 'drive-by art piece' which upon first acquain-tance needs to be spelt out letter by letter as a child would read. In this approach it shares much of the same spirit as Brossa's work at Velodròm d'Horta described on pages 156–7.

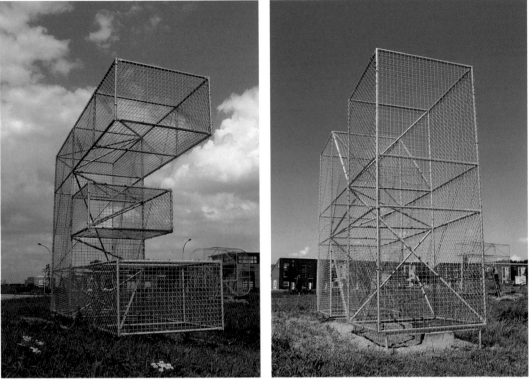

Artists & letters: 161
Maarten de Reus, *Groen*
in Carnisselande

162 **Recording: triumphalism, Rome, empire and dictatorship**

Roman emperors used space and architecture to remind the populace of their power. There are three triumphal arches in the vicinity of the Forum: from the north west to south east they were erected by Septimius Severus (AD203), Titus (AD81) and Constantine (AD315). Adorning the frieze of each is an inscription which now appears square cut, but which was originally infilled with bronze letters (see page 122). The holes for these are still visible. Opening with the formal dedication 'to the senate and people of Rome', these inscriptions go on to declare the achievements of each respective emperor yet, while the arches of both Titus and Constantine are dedicated to real empire-expanding achievements, the arch of Severus is more vain than most, in its celebration of little more than the anniversary of the Emperor's reign.

Such use of grand architecture to stir the imagination was also used by the Fascist dictator Mussolini between 1919 and 1943, and most of the best examples of this feature lettering as a significant element.

An early phase sees a revival of the seriffed Roman forms used in both antiquity and during the Renaissance period. In quoting from the ancient period they also feature *V* used instead of *U*.

These seriffed letterforms are used in two key buildings which form part of a new town begun in 1938 for the planned World's Fair of 1942. The district, whose master plan was conceived by Marcello Piacentini, is now known as EUR (the initials of Esposizione Universale di Roma).

The first, the Palazzo Uffizi EUR, has lettering in a single line reminiscent of Renaissance practice (see page 123). The lettering is not incised, but finished flush with a contrasting marble.

The most striking building, however, is the 'Square Colosseum' of 1938–40 (163/3) designed by

Giovanni Guerrini, Ernesto Bruno La Padula and Mario Romano. This is situated on a promontory overlooking the River Tiber and has lettering adorning all four sides. Using scale alone for impact, it proclaims:

A PEOPLE OF POETS OF ARTISTS OF HEROES OF SAINTS OF THINKERS OF SCIENTISTS OF NAVIGATORS OF EXPLORERS

The dreadful justification of the three lines is accentuated by the relationship of word and interlinear space but despite this, it still has the power and conviction to take your breath away.

Recording: triumphalism, Rome, empire and dictatorship

163

164 **Recording: triumphalism, Rome under Mussolini**

A second period of lettering style, from 1933 onwards, features sans serifs. Like the seriffed lettering at EUR, these too are characterized by the use of V instead of U and use Roman numerals – often counting the years from 1922 (the year in which Mussolini came to power) rather than from Christ's birth.

A chilly severity informs the geometry of the lettering on Arnaldo Foschini's church of SS Pietro e Paolo in EUR (164/1–2). Like the lettering on the Square Colosseum (see previous page), this also suffers from a lack of space between the lines and dreadful justification which has opened up huge word spaces.

In addition, although the lettering appears on the entablatures on all four sides of the building, it seems rather understated; a single line of letters would have been more in scale with this vast church and been far more effective.

On the Monument to the Garibaldini of 1941, designed by

Giovanni Jacobucci (164/3 & 165/1), the lettering is also derived from geometry but, like countless other examples from Spain, France and Portugal, this is interpreted in a far freer, more playful way. Typical of this southern European style are the enlarged bowls of the letters *P* & *R*, and the very low crossbar of *A*.

(See also examples on pages 136–7.)

At Piazza Augusto Imperatore, a building of 1940 has letterforms which have more in common with grotesque models and the overriding concern is not with legibility but with effect. Unlike both the Square Colosseum (see page 163) and SS Pietro e Paolo (164/1 & 2), the inscription here is centred not justified, and the resultant even word space is filled with a centre point in the manner of early Roman inscriptions. This, together with the smooth surface of the lettering raised above a textured background, allows the composition to read as one coherent whole.

**Recording: triumphalism, 165
Rome under Mussolini**

166 **Recording: triumphalism, Rome under Mussolini**

Foro Italico, the entrance to Mussolini's sporting complex, was built following Enrico Del Debbio's master plan of 1928, with alterations in 1931, 1933 and 1936. The final version was intended for the Olympic Games of 1944, and the stadium eventually hosted them in 1960, was remodelled for the football World Cup in 1990 and is now home to both Lazio and Roma.

On approaching from the Ponte Duca d'Aosta, an obelisk dated 'X' proclaims 'Mussolini Dux'. Beyond is a processional route whose pavement is one large mosaic. This contains scenes about the foundation of Rome and other historical events, as well as slogans. The lettering has much in common with that on the Monument to the Garibaldini (see page 164), and its rhythmic regularity is well suited to its use here: it has been likened to patterns echoing the chanting of a crowd.

Flanking the pavement are 24 marble blocks, eleven on each side facing the Tiber and one on each side (near the stadium) facing inward. All but the final three on the left are inscribed. The inscriptions begin with the story of the triumph of the Fascist regime from 1915 to 1936, and stones 12–18 are about the war and empire. These original Fascist inscriptions

are all shallow v-cut and vary slightly from one to the other. After the war, slabs 19–21 were cut in a slightly different style and tell the story of how the regime was defeated and Italy received a constitution.

Recording: triumphalism, Rome under Mussolini 167

168 Recording: triumphalism & reflection

The commemoration of battle has, in the tradition of triumphalism so well practiced by the Romans, been rather more partial in spirit in the past than is often the case now.

Thomas Telford's bridge on his Shrewsbury–Holyhead turnpike road in Wales is a splendid example of nineteenth-century triumphalism.

Built in 1815, this bridge is also known as the Waterloo Bridge owing to the text it bears, declaring: THIS ARCH WAS CONSTRUCTED IN THE SAME YEAR THE BATTLE OF WATERLOO WAS FOUGHT (and, by implication, one could almost add, 'and won').

Constructed from cast iron, the lettering, repeated on both sides, is in open-metal form, not dissimilar in effect to the balustrade lettering found at Castle Ashby (see page 126). The robust forms of the Clarendon letter are perfectly suited to their context and appear not so much to have been applied to the bridge but rather to be physically part of the structure.

168/3 shows a far simpler commemoration to battle. Proclaiming four victories of the Crimean War, (Inkerpol, Sebastopol and Alma are the other three), the use of the canon is certainly triumphal but is offset against the stark and somewhat unsettling incised and widely spaced sans serif letterforms.

VIERZIG
TAUSEND
SÖHNE
DER STADT
LIESSEN
IHR LEBEN
FÜR EUCH

1914 – 1918

THEIR

MEMORY

ENDURETH

FOR EVER

MARTYRS FRANÇAIS
DE LA DÉPORTATION

1945

More recent memorials to battle are no less monumental in sensibility yet, in the wake of the devastating wars of the twentieth century, they are more sombre, dedicated to the commemoration of injustice and the loss of life rather than to proclaiming victory (169/1 & 2). The German example (169/1) simply records that:

40,000 | SONS OF | THE CITY
LOST | THEIR LIVES
FOR YOU.

Lettering plays a key role in introducing the Monument to the Martyrs of the Deportation in Paris which itself is at a lower level and is reliant upon pattern and texture alone as tools of communication. The harsh and spiky letterforms are cut into the concrete walls and are made more dramatic still through the use of colour. Yet, the drama has not been overplayed, the fineness and overall lightness of the letterforms offsetting well the brutality of the concrete.

Recording: 169
triumphalism & reflection

170 **Recording: commemoration**

The scale of the major conflicts of the twentieth century has also brought about a change in the nature and locality of war memorials. The Caen Memorial (170/1 & 2) is a memorial to those who died during the Allied invasion of France, but it is also a visitor centre which explains what happened at that time and where in the area the sites of battle, other memorials and war grave are. Somehow it manages to achieve both aims with considerable dignity, the enormity of human cost being articulated by space, lighting and simple lettering.

The Holocaust memorial in Boston (170/3 & 4) makes use of a range of lettering techniques. The steel and glass structure is introduced and concluded by inscribed marble blocks. Metal grills on the floor then articulate the transition through the space, each incorporating the name of a particular concentration camp. The numbers of inmates are etched into the glass walls. In terms of execution all this is pretty standard fare – competent but a little self-aware and far from overwhelming. What is moving, however, is the simple act of recording, in this case by numbers not names, the millions of lives taken. It serves to remind us again of the resonance that text alone can have.

Recording: commemoration 171

The recording of hundreds or thousands of dead in war cemeteries also achieves a certain poignancy through the repetition of head-stones. In this cemetery in France (171/1), some distinction between faiths in the treatment of the graves at least bestows some sense of indi-viduality to those commemorated.

Ordinary graveyards provide an opportunity for a more individual commemoration of a life lived. The lettering on older stones show changing tastes combined with the individual interests of stone-cutters. For example, the larger letters of 171/3 combine aspects of both Egyptian and Clarendon forms.

Today most gravestones are soul-lessly mass-produced. A look at the traditions of other countries reveals the staleness of our own ideas, espe-cially concerning materials (171/4). Happily though, a revival of interest in hand lettering has more recently resulted in an increase in individu-ally considered stones (171/5).

PÅ DENNA PLATS MÖRDADES
SVERIGES
STATSMINISTER
OLOF PALME
DEN 28 FEBRUARI 1986

AJUNTAMENT
DE BARCELONA
EN RECONEIXEMENT
Camiseria
Bonet
1890   1993
ALS SEUS ANYS DE
SERVEI A LA CIUTAT

5 호선 Line
갈아타는곳
Transfer
김포공항 방화 방면
To Gimpo Airport Banghwa

5 호선 Line
갈아타는곳
Transfer
상일동 마천방면
To Sangil-dong Macheon

CLIFTON & COOPER
PAVIORS
&
ASPHALTERS
DUBLIN

1904
ABERTHAW CO CONCRETE
BOSTON
RANSOME PAT

172 **Incidentals: recording, instructing, advertising**

Lettering on the road itself is often used to reinforce instructions for drivers (see pages 62–3) but it can also be used in more visually subtle ways in a pedestrian context. Some of these are shown here and on the following six pages.

In a busy street, the ground sometimes proves the most most obvious place to record significant events or cultural locations (172/1 & 2), to give directions (172/3 & 4) or to state a manufacturer's name (172/5 & 6), for instance.

If such items are cast in concrete, as with the last two examples, lettering can be introduced in the form of a brass inlay which will be kept polished by pedestrian traffic. Where service covers are made from a slippery material, such as cast iron, there is the need to provide some form of grip, usually by creating a textured pattern. On the coal-hole covers outside Georgian or Victorian houses (172/1–6) advantage was often taken of this fact and a simple advertisement in the form of the manufacturer's name (and sometimes address) was used to create the required textured surface. In addition to their visual interest, these names can tell us much about the number of local manufacturers in a given town or city.

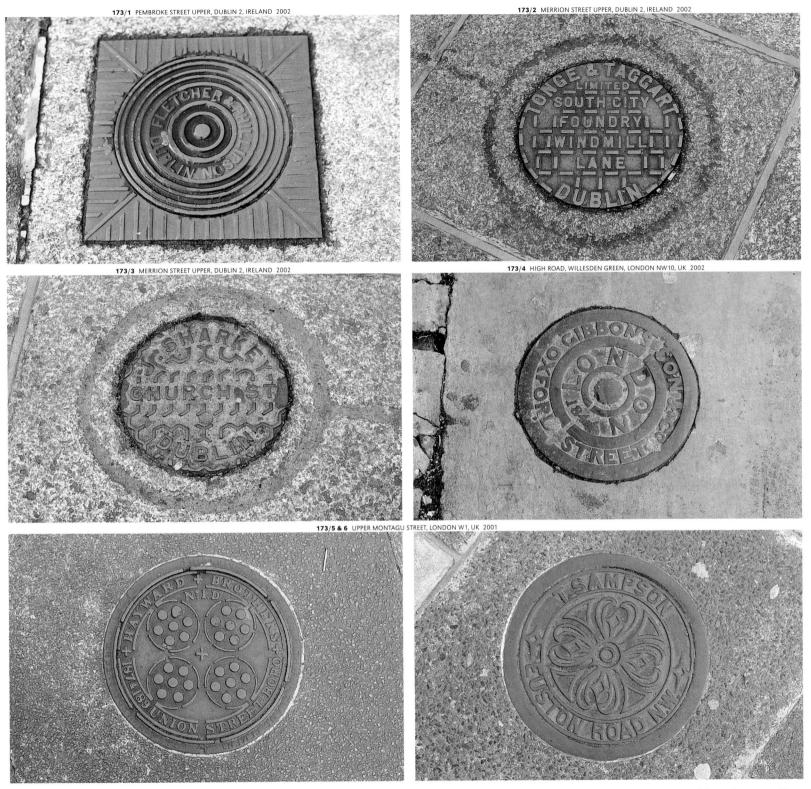

173/1 PEMBROKE STREET UPPER, DUBLIN 2, IRELAND 2002

173/2 MERRION STREET UPPER, DUBLIN 2, IRELAND 2002

173/3 MERRION STREET UPPER, DUBLIN 2, IRELAND 2002

173/4 HIGH ROAD, WILLESDEN GREEN, LONDON NW10, UK 2002

173/5 & 6 UPPER MONTAGU STREET, LONDON W1, UK 2001

174/3 WILLESDEN GREEN, LONDON NW10, UK 1992

174/4 CARRER DE ROGER DE FLOR, BARCELONA, SPAIN 2002

174/5 SAN LORENZO, FLORENCE, ITALY 1996

174/6 ST NICHOLAS STREET, KING'S LYNN, NORFOLK, UK 2001

174 Incidentals: recording, instructing, advertising

While there will always be the need or desire to make grand statements, it is often the small details which determine the visual texture and contribute to a sense of place.

The examples on this page are all utility markers. In each case, considerable care has been taken in making either a simple statement of their purpose, or in stating the company or manufacturer's name. Just as the coal-hole covers on the previous page carried the names of long gone manufacturers, 174/1 & 2 indicate suppliers now amalgamated into larger concerns, while 174/3 shows a once standard pattern now replaced by a mundane plastic alternative. While most examples shown can only state what lies behind or below, the form of 175/2, in addition to some unusual lettering, is particularly demonstrative.

Even in the first half of the twentieth century, it was possible for councils and even local builders to order manhole covers with their own name on from a local manufacturer (175/ 1). Today it tends only to be larger companies who customize standard products with their own name or design. With the changes in manufacturing practice throughout the twentieth century, the production of standard gratings and manhole

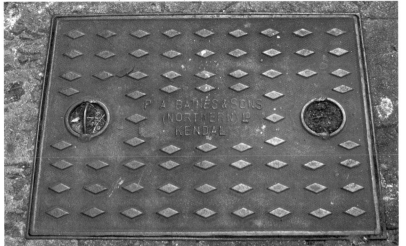

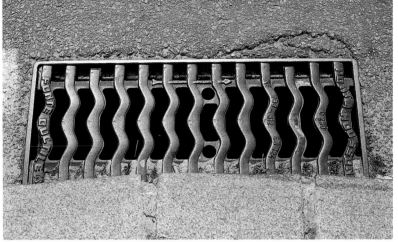

175/3 BARCELONA, SPAIN 2000

175/4 THESSALONIKI, GREECE 2002

175/5 PASSEIG DE GRÀCIA, BARCELONA, SPAIN 2002

175/6 BOSTON, MASSACHUSETTS, USA 1999

covers shows much less local diversity with only a handful of companies supplying such items throughout the whole of western Europe. The company which made 175/2, Pont-a-Mousson of France, is a partner in the multinational Compagnie à Saint-Gobain which owns major manufacturers in Britain, Germany, Italy, Portugal and Spain amongst other places. The bridge symbol or the initials PAM on a grating are becoming more and more commonplace.

Incidentals: recording, instructing, advertising 175

176/4 NEAR FARMERS' MARKET, LOS ANGELES, CALIFORNIA, USA 1992

176/5 OUTSIDE APREMONT CASTLE, VENDÉE, FRANCE 2001

176/6 PETALING JAYA, MALAYSIA 1998

176 Incidentals: recording, instructing, advertising

Many older examples of utility markers exist (176/1–3), and like the old road signs in Britain (see pages 20–1) or France (pages 40–3) their removal is quite unnecessary.

Elsewhere, items with lettering such as the time switch (176/4) or pump (176/5) seem to survive more by accident than design, but their presence adds to the unique experience of a place as well as telling us something about its history.

Occasionally, objects can be pressed into reuse, these ornamental plinths (176/6) support contemporary telephone kiosks, albeit in a somewhat incongruous manner.

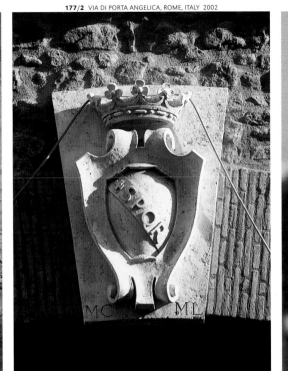

In Rome, the introductory words used on triumphal arches – Senatvs Popvlvs Qve Romanvs (to the Senate and people of Rome), see page 162 – were sometimes abbreviated to four letters: S, P, Q and R. These have since been used in what amounts to a corporate identity for the city in the same way that other cities use a coat of arms or some form of logotype.

What makes Rome interesting is that the essential aspect is the letters and not their form, and the diversity of objects which they adorn. This diversity is reflected in many different ways and materials to suit the style of an era or building, or the material they are made from (177/1–6).

Incidentals: 177
letters as identity, S P Q R

178/3 RAMBLA ST JOSEP 83, BARCELONA, SPAIN 2002

178/4 HORNCASTLE CHURCH, LINCOLNSHIRE, UK 1992

178/5 JOHN'S LANE WEST, DUBLIN 8, IRELAND 2002

178/6 MACKLIN STREET, LONDON WC2, UK 1997

**178 Incidentals:
dates & makers**

Although the motivation may be mixed, the desire to sign and date a piece of work of which you are proud goes back a long way.

The examples shown here range from the prominent and the extrovert to the almost invisible, and unlike the examples of lettering shown on the previous six pages, most of these require your eyes to be facing upwards.

In comparison to the dates shown here, recent attempts by developers to fulfil a similar purpose often fail because they exhibit no genuine understanding of letterforms or sympathy for materials.

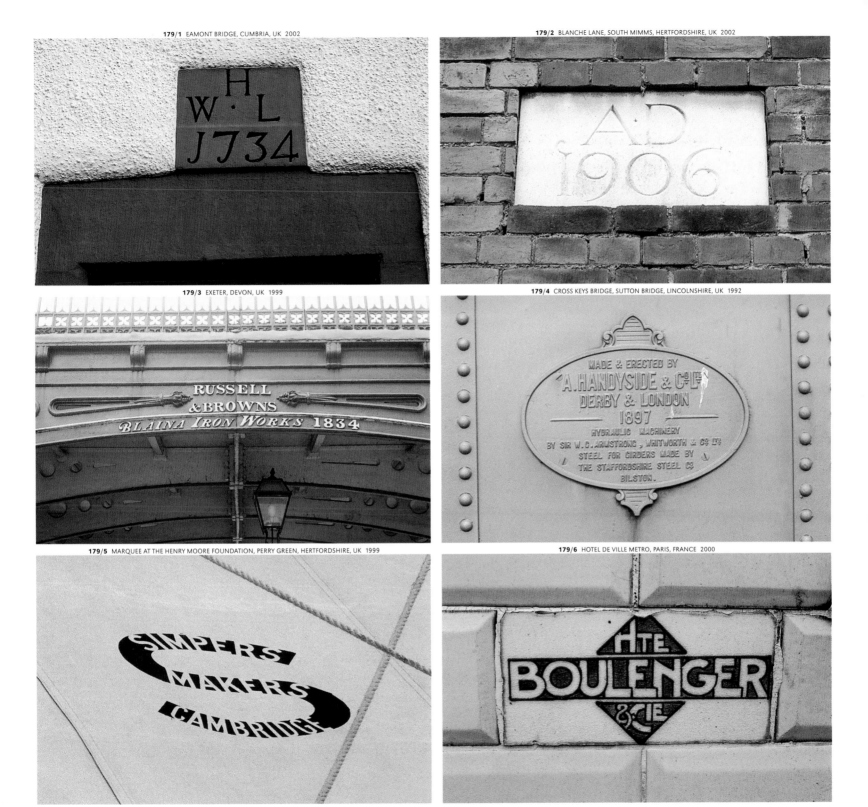

179/1 EAMONT BRIDGE, CUMBRIA, UK 2002

179/2 BLANCHE LANE, SOUTH MIMMS, HERTFORDSHIRE, UK 2002

179/3 EXETER, DEVON, UK 1999

179/4 CROSS KEYS BRIDGE, SUTTON BRIDGE, LINCOLNSHIRE, UK 1992

179/5 MARQUEE AT THE HENRY MOORE FOUNDATION, PERRY GREEN, HERTFORDSHIRE, UK 1999

179/6 HOTEL DE VILLE METRO, PARIS, FRANCE 2000

**Incidentals: 179
dates & makers**

180 **Twelve pictures which wouldn't fit anywhere else**   Some favourites, enough said.

181/4 ON STRADA NO.439 BETWEEN PONTEDERA AND VOLTERRA, ITALY 2002

181/5 RUE DU PÈRE-ETERNAL, AURAY, BRITTANY, FRANCE 2002

181/6 MÖLLE, SWEDEN 2002

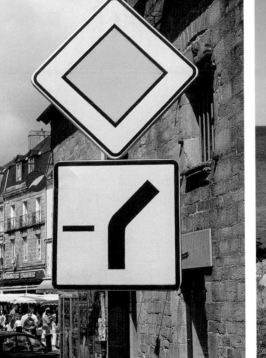

Twelve pictures which 181
wouldn't fit anywhere else

ESTRADA DO FAROL

←  Escadinhas

← Miradouro

← Ermida

← Escola

← Praia Carvalho

← Praia Vale Centeanes

← Praia Vale Covo

← Farol-Alfanzina

← Algar Seco

← Mercado

PERFUMARIA
COLONIA

RESTAURANTE CHINÊS
"Grande Muralha"
長城   Tel. 357380

Glossary 1: parts of a letter

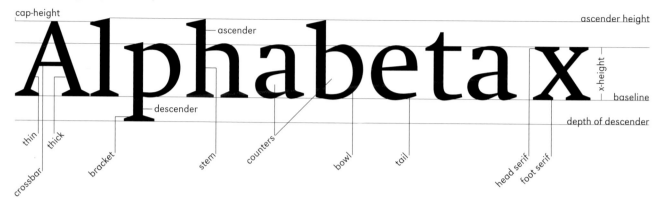

cap-height • ascender height • ascender • x-height • baseline • depth of descender • thin • thick • crossbar • bracket • stem • counters • bowl • tail • head serif • foot serif

Glossary 2: terms, materials & techniques

Italics refer to other glossary entries, **bold** to photographs.

Anderson (Sir Colin) Chairman of the committee which advised British parliament on traffic signs for motorways. Its findings, published in 1962 (see Sources & further reading), were accepted and introduced immediately. See pages 24–5.

Architectural ceramics A broad term covering all building materials made from fired clay. While including bricks, chimney pots, etc., for our purposes it is limited to three main kinds: terracotta, faience and tiles. Both *terracotta* and *faience* are used to describe three-dimensional hollow blocks, cast from a mould, which can – when filled with concrete – form structural elements and be used with brick or other building materials. When unglazed (or with a transparent glaze) these are known as terracotta, see **118/1–2**. (Below, Hanway Place, London W1, UK 1992.)

When glazed they are known as faience (after the Italian town of Faenza, an important centre for glazed pottery). See **80/2** & **84/5–6**. (Below, Paris Metro, France 2000.)

Tiles Thin, flat pieces of glazed or unglazed clay used as a floor- or wall-covering and are not, strictly speaking, part of the building fabric. See **138/1–2**. (Below, Tynemouth Station, Tyne & Wear, UK 1982.)

Casting A process used to create any design or pattern by using a mould. Such a pattern may be in relief (raised) or reverse cast (impressed). Typical materials used in this process are iron (see **20/1–6** & **173/1–6**), concrete (see **132/1–133/3**) and bronze (see **134/4–135/3**). (Below: one of the moulds for **131/2**, 2002.)

Carving The process of creating a design in wood or stone by cutting, usually with a chisel and dummy (round-headed hammer). A design can be formed by cutting the subject itself, when it is known as incised (see also *cut*). See **106/1–107/6** & **122/1 & 3**. (Below, Bath, Wiltshire, UK 2002.)

When the background is cut away, the design is referred to as being in relief (see also *section*). See **120/3–4** & **127/1–6.** (Below, Sticklandgate, Kendal, Cumbria, UK 2001.)

Clarendon A form of *slab-serif* letter with bracketed serifs. Generally square in proportion, with an evenness of character width and noticeable contrast between thicks and thins, this sturdy letter first appears in the early nineteenth century, though the slightly condensed typeform first registered in that name, and which was to become the norm, doesn't actually appear until 1845. See **142/1** & **168/1–2** and *Egyptian*. (Below, locomotive 55015 at King's Cross Station, London, UK 1979.)

Curvilinear Letterforms, usually seriffed, with an organic or ornamental restlessness of form and exaggerated in curve and proportion: bowls to the letters *B*, *D*, *P* & *R* may swell and crossbars of *A*, *E*, *F* & *H* may be set either very high or very low rather than just above centre. See **80/1–3** & **118/2**. (Below, Kingsway, London WC2, UK, 2002)

Cut Term used to describe the shape of a slice through a three-dimensional letterform when incised or impressed. Typical cut shapes include *V-cut*, see **121/1–2** (below, Tavistock Street, London WC2, UK 2002)

and *square-cut*, see **120/6** (below, Durham Cathedral, UK 1993).

DIN Deutsches Institut für Normung, the German equivalent of the British Standards Institute (BSI). Both publish national standards and are members of the International Standards Organization (ISO) and Comité Européen de Normalisation (CEN).

Dot-matrix A restricted grid from which letters can be rendered, typically by lights. See **93/1–3**. (Below, Marylebone Station London NW1, UK 2002.)

Egyptian A form of slab-serif letter whose serifs are unbracketed. Generally square in proportion, with an evenness of character width and line, this sturdy letter first appears early in the nineteenth century and as a typeform around 1817. See **142/3** and Clarendon. (Below, Tuesday Market, King's Lynn, Norfolk, UK 2001.)

Enamelling see vitreous stove enamelling

English letter A vernacular interpretation of the Roman square capital which originated in the mid-eighteenth century. Fully evolved, it is robust and square in proportion with capitals almost uniform in width. Contrast between thicks and thins is strong, forms are full and rounded with serifs generously bracketed. See **105/1** & **121/2** and compare with the Roman Trajan letter. The solid underlying proportions of the 'English letter' also inform many nineteenth-century Clarendon, Egyptian and grotesque letterforms and types. (Below, Wilton, Wiltshire, UK 1998.)

Etching A process whereby a design is interpreted as a relief surface using acid as the agent, typically on metal plates used for printing, but also widely used on glass and other surfaces for decorative purposes. See **170/4**. (Below, All Saints' Church, Holbeach, Lincolnshire, UK 2002.)

Faience see architectural ceramics

Fascia A narrow definition would be the clearly defined area on the front of a commercial premises on which to install a sign. Such signs may be regarded as temporary and are not integral to a building's structure. See pages 119 & 136–7. In this book we also refer to other architecturally non-integral lettering as 'fascia'. (Below, Museum Street, London WC1, UK 1995.)

Finger posts Signposts with thin arms radiating from a pole and pointing towards the stated destination. See **20/1–21/6** & **66/1–67/3**. (Below, near Spalding, Lincolnshire, UK 2002.)

Geneva Protocol Agreement about the standardization of road signs reached at the 1949 United Nations conference on road and motor transport held in Geneva. See pages 47–57.

Glass A material which can be etched or stained with designs to contrast with its usual transparent state. Often used for fascias when it is frequently seen with lettering or other designs painted and/or gilded on its reverse. See **119/2** & **136/1–6**. (Below, Exeter, Devon, UK 1999.)

Grotesque A sans serif letter of the nineteenth century, appearing as type from the 1830s. It is characterized by a sturdy squareness of form, evenness of character width and often, when used architecturally, an evenness of line. See **124/3** & **143/1**. (Below, Mercer Row, Louth, Lincolnshire, UK 1992.)

Heritage styling The styling of signs and other street furniture to make them appear old and 'fit' better in conservation areas. Too often, however, such imitation is only an approximation of historical models and ignores the size, mass and detailing of actual surviving examples. See **66/1–3**, **67/1** & **113/2**. (Below, old and new in Albert Road, London NW1, UK 2002.)

Illumination Lighting can draw attention to existing signs by floodlighting, or by backlighting a sign made of transparent material. Smaller lighting elements can be installed inside three-dimensional letters. See **145/3–6** (Below, Clacton-on-Sea, Essex, UK 2002.)

Tubular lighting elements such as neon can be used to create the actual shape of the lettering itself. See **145/1–2 & 5**. (Below, West Central Street, London WC1, UK 1995.)

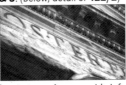

Infilling Practice of filling carved or reverse-cast letters with a contrasting medium. See **163/1 & 3**. (Below, detail of **122/2**)

Informatory signs provide information as opposed to definite instructions. Such information is often directional. See pages 16–46 and regulatory signs. (Below, Tottenham Court Road, London W1, UK c.1969)

Letter spacing see spacing

Makers' marks Akin to a signature on a painting, a record of designer, architect or manufacturer, sometimes a prominent feature (see **173/1–6**), sometimes more discreet (see **20/3 & 6**). (Below, RMS Queen Mary, Long Beach, California, USA 1992.)

Map-type sign Directional sign, usually for motor traffic, in which the road ahead is represented as a map with straight ahead at the top. See **26/1** & **29/1–5** and stack-type sign. (Below, Harrow Road, London W2, UK 2002.)

Michelin French tyre company founded in 1889 which erected around 70,000 ceramic signs around France between 1931 and 1970. See pages 40–3. (Below, St Maixent-sur-Vie, Vendée, France 2001.)

Milestone Generic name for stones, posts, plaques or other markers used to indicate the passage of distance, and other related information, along a particular route. See pages 16–18. (Below, B556 [previously A6], Hertfordshire, UK 2002.)

Other countries (notably France) have kilometre stones serving the same purpose, see page 19.

Mosaic The arrangement of small pieces of glass, tile or other materials to create a picture or pattern. See **138/3–6** & **139/2, 5 & 6**. (Below, Long Acre, London WC1, UK 1995.)

Neon see *illumination*

Painting Perhaps the most basic way of applying lettering or other decoration to walls. Older, lead-based, paints have a surprising longevity. See **143/1–4**. (Below, Wardrobe Place, London EC4, UK 2000.)

Pictogram As its name suggests, a 'pictorial diagram' often used to convey simple information about facilities, etc. without the need for written information. See **87/3** & **89/1–6**. (Below, Shanghai, China 2002.)

Regulatory signs govern (road) users' behaviour by giving definite instructions. If a sign system adheres to the Geneva Protocol of 1949 these instructions are reinforced by the use of signs of differing shapes for positive or negative instructions, see pages 47–57 and *informatory signs*. (Below, Warwick Avenue, London W2, UK 2002)

Roman square capital A formal letter characterized by a square-ness to its widest characters, though an underlying sense of geometry establishes a pattern for characters of differing widths (eg, *M* & *O* occupy a square while *B* & *L* only half a square). Any geometric references are, how-ever, softened by the influence of the brush/pen which results in forms gently modulated in line. See pages 122–3.

(Below, Piazza San Giovanni in Laterano, Rome, Italy, 2002.)

Roman Trajan letter Form of *Roman square capital* found on Trajan's Column of AD 113 and widely lauded as exemplary. Following Edward Johnston's influence it was used as model for much public carved work throughout the twentieth century. See **120/1**. (Below, Louth, Lincolnshire, UK 1992.)

Sans serif A letter without serifs or other terminal strokes. The basic idea of the sans serif form has been widely interpreted, for example, a particular nineteenth century interpretation of sans serif is identified as *grotesque*. See also *Swiss typefaces*. (Below, Grand Canal Docks, Dublin 4, Ireland 2002.)

Section Term used to describe the shape of a slice through a three-dimensional letterform when in relief. See **120/3–4**. Some typical sectional shapes are shown below.
Square-section, (below, Market Place, Wisbech, Cambridgeshire, UK 2002).

Round-section, (below, Exchange Street, Dublin, Ireland 2002).

Siesta S Our term for the relaxed, forward-sloping *S* found in some examples of sans-serif lettering, especially, though not exclusively, in Southern Europe. See **137/3**. (Below, Barcelona, Spain 2000.)

Silhouette Letters cut-out or in relief seen against a background of contrasting colour or material. While no longer permitted in the UK, in some countries, use is made of the skyline to heighten the effect. (Below, Boston, Massachusetts, USA 1999.)

Slab-serif Heavy rectangular serif which can be bracketed to the main stem (*Clarendon*) or be un-bracketed (*Egyptian*). (Below, Willesden [not *in situ*], London NW10, UK 1992.)

Spacing Legibility of any text is reliant on the spacing between letters, words and lines as much as the shapes of the characters themselves. A constant space between words in a line helps the flow of reading and should not appear greater than the space between lines ('leading') unless texture, not legibility, is the goal. Increasing the space between letters can greatly increase the legibility of words needed to be read at distance or when white letters are on a dark background.

Square-cut see *cut*
Square section see *section*
Stack-type sign Information sign, usually directional, in which the information appears as a list. The grouping of information may be further articulated by the use of separate panels. See **27/1** & **45/1–3** and *map-type sign*. (Below, Carvoeiro, Portugal, 1996.)

Stencil A thin sheet with a cut-out design which is transferred onto another surface by means of paint etc. In its typical form, letters created by this method are characterized by being made up of discontinuous elements. See **63/3, 4 & 6**. (Below, a skip in Paris, France 2000)

Stucco An external render of plaster or cement which was often moulded to resemble dressed stonework, or cast with decorative designs or lettering. See **120/6** & **142/1**. (Below detail of **105/1**, 2003.)

Swiss typefaces *Sans serifs* such as Helvetica and similar fonts.
Temporary see *fascia*
Terracotta see *architectural ceramics*
Tiles see *architectural ceramics*
Transport alphabet Typeface in two weights designed by Jock Kinneir and Margaret Calvert for the British road sign system in 1963, still in use. (Below, Transport Medium, detail of figure 2 of the *Worboys* report.)

Trompe l'oeil A painted or other two-dimensional representation designed to create the illusion of three dimensions. See **136/4**. (Below, Clacton-on-Sea, Essex, UK 2002.)

Utility markers A grille, post, etc. which indicates the presence of services such as gas, electricity or water. See pages 173–6. (Below, Boston, Massachusetts, USA 1999)

Vernacular Traditions to have emerged from regional practice and, as related to architecture, usually concerned with the ordinary rather than the monumental, see pages 124–5. Also used here to refer to untutored practice of a much broader kind. (Below, Clacton-on-Sea, Essex, UK 2002.)

Vitreous stove enamelling A process whereby designs in coloured powdered glass, either dry or as an ink, are transferred, by means of *stencils*, transfers or screen-printing, onto sheet steel or iron. These are fused onto the sheet by firing in a furnace at temperatures of around 800–860°C. See **110/1–5**. (Below, Paris, France 2000.)

Worboys (Sir Walter) Chairman of the committee which advised the British parliament on traffic signs for all-purpose roads. Its findings, published in 1963 (see Sources & further reading) were accepted and introduced from 1964 onwards. See pages 26–31.

Word space see *spacing*
Wrought iron Iron which has been heated then hammered, stretched and twisted into shape, usually by hand. Today much reproduction work actually uses mild steel bars. See **140/3** & **141/3**. (Below, Paris, France 2000.)

Sources & further reading

Essential books

Alan **Bartram**, *Lettering in architecture*, London, Lund Humphries 1975
Nicolete **Gray**, *Lettering on buildings*, London, Architectural Press & New York, Reinhold 1960
Jock **Kinneir**, *Words and buildings: the art and practice of public lettering*, London, Architectural Press 1980

General

Patrick **Baglee** (ed.), *Open air*, London, G F Smith 1999
Phil **Baines**, 'Letterforms: history, values, possibilities' *Point* 8 (Art & Design Research Journal) 1999/2000, pp.5–13
Phil **Baines** & Catherine **Dixon**, 'Letter-rich Lisbon', *Eye* 56, Summer 2005, pp.52–61
—, 'Sheffield: a sense of place', *Eye* 58, Winter 2005, pp.56–64
Alan **Bartram**, *The English lettering tradition from 1700 to the present day*, London, Lund Humphries 1986
Peter **Campbell**, 'Reading the signs', *London Review of Books* 24, Vol.24, 12 December 2002, p.28
Richard **Dragun** 'Where are you, where you've been and where you're going', *Typographic writing* (ed. David Jury), Stroud, ISTD 2001, pp.66–9
Edward **Fella**, *Letters on America*, London, Laurence King 2000
Milner **Gray** & Ronald **Armstrong**, *Lettering for architects & designers*, London, B T Batsford 1962
James **Grayson Truelove**, *This way: signage design for public spaces*, Gloucester, MA, Rockport 2000
Georges **Jean**, *Signs, symbols and ciphers: decoding the message*, London, Thames & Hudson 1998
Robert **Massin**, *Letter and image*, London, Studio Vista 1970
Steven **Rothfeld** & André **Aciman**, *Entrez: signs of France*, New York, Artisan 2000
America **Sanchez**, *Barcelona grafica*, Barcelona, Gili 2001
Fred **Smeijers**, 'Typography versus commercial lettering', *TypoGraphic* 54 (Journal of the International Society of Typographic Designers), August 1999, pp.15–18. Reprinted in *Typographic writing* (ed. David Jury) Stroud, ISTD 2001, pp.147–51
The magazine *Typographica* – edited and designed by Herbert Spencer and published by Lund Humphries between 1949 and 1967 – devoted many pages to subjects covered in this book.

Among the most pertinent (all from the 'new series') are
Alan **Bartram**, 'Spanish street lettering', no.15, 1967
Nicolete **Gray**, 'Lettering in Coventry Cathedral', no.6, 1962
James **Mosley**, 'The nymph and the grot, the revival of the san-serif letter', no.12, 1965
Anthony **Robinson**, 'Letters underfoot', no.7, 1963
Herbert **Spencer**, 'Mile-a-minute typography', no.7, 1963
Edward **Wright**, 'Emphatic fist, informative arrow', no.12, 1965
Margaret **Wissing**, 'Road signs in Holland', no.12, 1965
Illustrations of some of the above, together with a full history of the magazine, can be found in Rick **Poynor**, *Typographica*, London, Laurence King 2001

On signs & information

Peter **Barker** & June **Fraser**, *Sign design guide, a guide to inclusive signage*, London, JMU and the Sign Design Society 2000.
Peter **Bil'ak**, 'Stereotypes on the streets, or In search of Mr Ligac', *Dot Dot Dot* 3, Summer 2001
Crosby, Fletcher, Forbes, *A sign systems manual*, London, Studio Vista 1970
James **Sutton**, *Signs in action*, London, Studio Vista 1965
Peter **Wildbur**, *Information graphics: a survey of typographic, diagrammatic and cartographic communication*, London, Trefoil 1989

Roads

Know your traffic signs, London, HMSO 1995
Traffic signs regulations, London, HMSO 1994
'Which signs for motorways?' *Design* 129, September 1959, pp.28–32
Sir Colin **Anderson** (Chair) *Motorway signs, final report of advisory committee on traffic signs for motorways*, HMSO 1962
Phil **Baines**, 'A design (to sign roads by)', *Eye* 34, Winter 1999, pp.26–36
Phil **Baines** & Catherine **Dixon**, 'The changing roadscape', *Forum* 9 (Journal of Letter Exchange), Autumn 2003, pp.6–9
Barry **Barton**, 'Signs of their times', *Cycle touring & campaigning* (magazine of the Cyclists' Touring Club) October/November 1996. pp.12–13
Mervyn **Benford**, *Milestones*, Princes Risborough, Shire 2002
Anthony **Froshaug**,' Roadside traffic signs', *Design* 178, October 1963, pp.37–50
Stuart **Hands**, *Road signs*, Princes Risborough, Shire 2002
H **Hutchison**, A W **Christie** &

K S **Rutley**, 'Lettering & legibility', *Design* 152, August 1961, pp.56–61
Robin **Kinross**, 'Road signs, wrong turning', *Blueprint* 61, October 1989, pp.50–2 and reprinted in Robin Kinross, *Unjustified texts, perspectives on typography*, London, Hyphen Press 2002
J **Thirot**, 'De la signalisations routes', *Arts et Metiers Graphiques Paris* 22, Quinze Mars 1931, pp.189–92
Walter **Worboys** (Chair) *Traffic signs 1963, report of the committee on traffic signs for all-purpose roads*, London, HMSO 1963

Railways

Phil **Baines** & Catherine **Dixon**, 'Variety & identity', *Druk* 2, Autumn 1999, Fontshop Benelux. pp.12–13
James **Cousins**, *British Rail design*, Copenhagen, Dansk Designråd & London, Design Council 1986
Brian **Haresnape**, *British Rail, a journey by design 1948–78*, London, Ian Allan 1979
Justin **Howes**, *Johnston's Underground types*, Harrow, Capital Transport 2000
David **Lawrence**, *Underground architecture*, Harrow, Capital Transport 1994

Specific subjects or issues

Alan **Bartram**, *Fascia lettering in the British Isles*, London, Lund Humphries & New York, Watson-Guptill 1978
—, *Street name lettering in the British Isles*, London, Lund Humphries & New York, Watson-Guptill 1978
—, *Tombstone lettering in the British Isles*, London, Lund Humphries & New York, Watson-Guptill 1978
Silvano **Fassina**, *Roman capitals, five itineraries in Rome*, Seattle, Legacy of Letters 1997
James **Mosley**, *The nymph and the grot, the revival of the san serif letter*, London, Friends of St Bride Printing Library 1999
John R **Nash**, 'In defence of the roman letter', *Edward Johnston Foundation Journal* 7, Autumn 2002, pp.3–22
Frances **Procter** & Philippa **Miller**, *Village and town signs in Norfolk*, Norwich, published by the authors 1973
Percy **Smith**, *Lettering, a plea*, London, First Edition Club 1932
Minos **Zarifopoulos**, 'Visual cleaning in Athens, an urban facelift challenges the Greek city's visual mosaic', *Eye* 45, Autumn 2002, pp.42–7

Artists' approaches

Phil **Baines**, 'Sculptured letters and public poetry', *Eye* 37, 2000, pp.38–49
Manuel **Guerrero** (ed.) *Joan*

Brossa, o la revuelta poética, Barcelona, Department de Cultura de la Generalitat de Catalunya, Fundació Joan Brossa & Fundació Joan Miró 2001

Basil **Spence**, *Phoenix at Coventry*, London, Geoffrey Bles 1962

Techniques

Christopher **Baglee** & Andrew **Morley**, *Street jewellery, a history of enamel advertising signs*, London, New Cavendish 1978

Percy J **Delf Smith**, *Civic and memorial lettering*, London, A & C Black 1946

Michael **Harvey**, *Creative lettering today*, London, A & C Black 1996

David **Kindersley** & Lida **Lopes Cardozo**, *Letters slate cut, workshop philosophy and practice in the making of letters, a sequel*, Cambridge, Cardoza Kindersley Editions 1990

Alan **May**, 'Roman bronze inscriptional lettering, a note on methods of production', *Typography Papers* 1, University of Reading, Department of Typography & Graphic Communication 1996, pp.123–9

Hans **van Lemmen**, *Architectural ceramics*, Princes Risborough, Shire 2002

Websites

A search using Google for any subject covered in the book will render many websites, some useful and carefully researched, others less so. The following list includes only those sites that we have consulted for certain parts of the book.

www.architecturaliron.com
www.centralletteringrecord.org
www.forgotten-ny.com
www.joanbrossa.org
www.milestone-society.org
www.milestonesweb.com
www.publiclettering.org.uk
www.route40.net
www.subirachs.org
www.tilesoc.org.uk

Index

Numbers in **bold** are photographs

Copyright © 2003
Phil Baines & Catherine Dixon

First published in Great Britain in 2003

This paperback edition first published in 2008 by
Laurence King Publishing Ltd
361-373 City Road
London EC1V 1LR
T +44 20 7841 6900
F +44 20 7841 6910
E enquiries@laurenceking.co.uk
www.laurenceking.co.uk

A catalogue record for this book is available from the British Library

ISBN 978-1-85669-576-3

Design (excluding cover) & picture research by the authors. Typeset in **Doctor**, Calvert & URW Grotesk

Cover design by Pentagram

Printed in Thailand

Photographic credits

All photography by the authors was shot on Pentax K-series cameras, with 28mm, 55mm and 75–250mm lenses. Our primary aim has always been to record the lettering first and make pictures second. This partly accounts for the variable lighting conditions, but we have long since learnt that you must photograph examples when you see them, as they may not be there when you return.

Additional photography by **Jackie Baines** 45/2; **Central Lettering Record** Phil Baines 131/1, 132/1–3, 133/1, 1351 & 2, 156/1–6, 157, 158/2–5, 159/1 & 3–5; Nicholas Biddulph 30/1, 86/1 & 2, 185/informatory; Juan Sebastián Martínez-Campos 159/2; **Niklas Dahlbeck** 52/2, 53/6, 55/4, 60/6, 61/1, 63/2, 79/4; **Michael Evidon** 37/2, 46/3, 56/5, 58/3, 62/3, 76/2, 144/2; **Michael Evidon & Mia Nilsson** 10–11, 181/6; **Lisa Ferneyhough** 35/1 & 2, 48/6, 49/1, 51/4 & 5, 52/1, 60/2. 77/1, 112/5; **Youseon Gang** 49/4, 57/1, 77/3, 89–90, 172/3; **G·Net** (courtesy Stephen Raw) 152/1; **Ben Hughes** 76/6, 89/3 & 4, 186/pictogram; **Robin Kinross** 171/6; **Amanda Lester** 181/4; **Janice Lo** 38/2, 52/6, 53/5, 62/1, 112/3; **Basia Pacześna** 46/4, 79/3, 89/5 & 6, 112/6; **Maarten de Reus** 162–3; **Kosuke Shikata** 19/6, 56/3, 57/4, 59/2, 60/1, 62/2; **Jason Skowronek** 79/1 & 2, 169/1; **Stefania Trofino** 49/3 & 5, 52/5, back cover/flap; **Jack Schulze** 127/6; **Minos Zarifopoulos** 119/5 & 6.

Glossary 1 is adapted from Phil Baines & Andrew Haslam, *Type & typography*, London, Laurence King 2001, p.38.

Acknowledgements

Our involvement with the Central Lettering Record (the teaching archive established at the Central School by Nicholas Biddulph and Nicolete Gray in the 1960s) has been a source of encouragement while pursuing our own interests in this field.

We have written articles for various magazines which have helped to clarify our thoughts. Our thanks to John Walters at *Eye*, Jan Midendorp & Catherine Dal at *Druk*, Alan & Isabella Livingstone at *Point*. In a similar way, Jack Schulze, Matt Hyde & George Agnelli, the designers and technical brains behind *Publiclettering.org*, also served to push our ideas both in writing and through photography.

Many other people have also given help and advice over the years, chief among these are Mike Ashworth of London's Transport Museum; Alan Bartram; Margaret Calvert; Richard Hollis; Robin Kinross; Brian Lyus; James Mosley; Paul Shaw; many members of ATypI and Letter Exchange; colleagues at Central Saint Martins, especially Sylvia Backemeyer, Stuart Evans, Geoff Fowle, Maziar Raien and Andrew Whittle.

Finally, our thanks to the people who in very practical ways have made this book possible, to all our students who kindly took photographs in the many places in the world we ourselves could not get to; to Ben Hughes for the same; to Malcolm Parker for his patient technical support and at Laurence King, Jo Lightfoot and Cleia Barton.

Dedication

To our respective families and friends who have in turn been
tolerant,
encouraging
and bemused.